New Directions for
Student Services

Susan R. Jones
Co-Editor

Sherry K. Watt
Co-Editor

College Student Mental Health

Heidi Levine
Susan R. Stock
Editors

Number 156 • Winter 2016
Jossey-Bass
San Francisco

New Directions for Student Services, no. 156

Co-Editors: Susan R. Jones and Sherry K. Watt

NEW DIRECTIONS FOR STUDENT SERVICES, (Print ISSN: 0164-7970; Online ISSN: 1536-0695), is published quarterly by Wiley Subscription Services, Inc., a Wiley Company, 111 River St., Hoboken, NJ 07030-5774 USA.

Postmaster: Send all address changes to NEW DIRECTIONS FOR STUDENT SERVICES, John Wiley & Sons Inc., C/O The Sheridan Press, PO Box 465, Hanover, PA 17331 USA.

Information for subscribers
New Directions for Student Services is published in 4 issues per year. Institutional subscription prices for 2017 are:
Print & Online: US$454 (US), US$507 (Canada & Mexico), US$554 (Rest of World), €359 (Europe), £284 (UK). Prices are exclusive of tax. Asia-Pacific GST, Canadian GST/HST and European VAT will be applied at the appropriate rates. For more information on current tax rates, please go to www.wileyonlinelibrary.com/tax-vat. The price includes online access to the current and all online backfiles to January 1st 2013, where available. For other pricing options, including access information and terms and conditions, please visit www.wileyonlinelibrary.com/access.

Delivery Terms and Legal Title
Where the subscription price includes print issues and delivery is to the recipient's address, delivery terms are **Delivered at Place (DAP)**; the recipient is responsible for paying any import duty or taxes. Title to all issues transfers FOB our shipping point, freight prepaid. We will endeavour to fulfil claims for missing or damaged copies within six months of publication, within our reasonable discretion and subject to availability.

Back issues: Single issues from current and recent volumes are available at the current single issue price from cs-journals@wiley.com.

Disclaimer
The Publisher and Editors cannot be held responsible for errors or any consequences arising from the use of information contained in this journal; the views and opinions expressed do not necessarily reflect those of the Publisher and Editors, neither does the publication of advertisements constitute any endorsement by the Publisher and Editors of the products advertised.

Publisher: New Directions for Student Services is published by Wiley Periodicals, Inc., 350 Main St., Malden, MA 02148-5020.

Journal Customer Services: For ordering information, claims and any enquiry concerning your journal subscription please go to www.wileycustomerhelp.com/ask or contact your nearest office.
Americas: Email: cs-journals@wiley.com; Tel: +1 781 388 8598 or +1 800 835 6770 (toll free in the USA & Canada).
Europe, Middle East and Africa: Email: cs-journals@wiley.com; Tel: +44 (0) 1865 778315.
Asia Pacific: Email: cs-journals@wiley.com; Tel: +65 6511 8000.
Japan: For Japanese speaking support, Email: cs-japan@wiley.com.
Visit our Online Customer Help available in 7 languages at www.wileycustomerhelp.com/ask

Production Editor: Shreya Srivastava (email: shsrivastava@wiley.com).

Wiley's Corporate Citizenship initiative seeks to address the environmental, social, economic, and ethical challenges faced in our business and which are important to our diverse stakeholder groups. Since launching the initiative, we have focused on sharing our content with those in need, enhancing community philanthropy, reducing our carbon impact, creating global guidelines and best practices for paper use, establishing a vendor code of ethics, and engaging our colleagues and other stakeholders in our efforts. Follow our progress at www.wiley.com/go/citizenship

View this journal online at wileyonlinelibrary.com/journal/ss

Wiley is a founding member of the UN-backed HINARI, AGORA, and OARE initiatives. They are now collectively known as Research4Life, making online scientific content available free or at nominal cost to researchers in developing countries. Please visit Wiley's Content Access - Corporate Citizenship site: http://www.wiley.com/WileyCDA/Section/id-390082.html

Printed in the USA by The Sheridan Group.

Address for Editorial Correspondence: Co-editors Susan R. Jones, and Sherry K. Watt, New Directions for Student Services, Email: jones.1302@osu.edu And sherry-watt@uiowa.edu

Abstracting and Indexing Services
The Journal is indexed by Academic Search Alumni Edition (EBSCO Publishing); Education Index/Abstracts (EBSCO Publishing); ERA: Educational Research Abstracts Online (T&F); ERIC: Educational Resources Information Center (CSC); Higher Education Abstracts (Claremont Graduate University).

Cover design: Wiley
Cover Images: © Lava 4 images | Shutterstock

For submission instructions, subscription and all other information visit:
wileyonlinelibrary.com/journal/ss

CONTENTS

Editors' Notes

In recent years there has been heightened attention paid to the mental health needs of college students, the range and scope of these issues, and the challenges related to the provision of mental health services. Mental health generally refers to students' psychological and emotional well-being and the conditions that affect their state of health, happiness, and security. Counseling center data, changing legal mandates, and anecdotal reports from senior practitioners all point to the growing complexity of managing these issues (e.g., Center for Collegiate Mental Health, 2016; Office of Civil Rights, 2010). Attend any meeting of senior student affairs officers and you are sure to hear discussion about how colleagues are handling such issues as managing students with inappropriate social behavior, challenges with special student populations, worries about suicidal or (potentially more worrisome) homicidal students, and simply keeping pace with rising needs in the face of limited resources. Barriers to effectively addressing student mental health issues may include a siloed approach that suggests these issues are the sole responsibility of the campus counseling professionals or a lack of knowledge about how licensed counselors and psychologist might effectively intervene in these situations. One of the goals of this volume is to suggest that student mental health is everyone's business—it certainly affects us all. Therefore, it is to both university student and employee benefit that campus administrators gain knowledge and skills that can directly and effectively address mental health issues on campus.

Throughout this volume we use the term "mental health" to speak in the broadest sense about students' psychological and emotional well-being. In many of the chapters, the authors distinguish "mental health issues" (situations that may reflect some disruption in students' optimal functioning) from "mental illness" or "disorders." The latter terms are used in those specific situations in which an individuals' functioning is sufficiently impaired as to constitute a condition in which some form of treatment or intervention may be appropriate.

Although a number of existing publications provide either skills focus for counselors-in-training or guidance for licensed counselors and psychologists working with college students, there are fewer resources for student affairs administrators interested in mental health issues. Reynolds' (2008) *Helping College Students* is primarily a textbook for graduate students in higher education/student affairs, with a focus on teaching about helping skills. Kadison and DiGeronimo's (2005) *College of the Overwhelmed* provides an overview of the types of mental health issues students experience and ways in which colleges might meet their needs; however, *Overwhelmed* focuses on the provision of clinical services, and its primary target audience was students and their families. A 2006 NASPA publication, *College Student*

New Directions for Student Services, no. 156, Winter 2016 © 2016 Wiley Periodicals, Inc.
Published online in Wiley Online Library (wileyonlinelibrary.com) • DOI: 10.1002/ss.20186

Mental Health (Benton & Benton, 2006), had an intended audience of practitioners and addressed how programs and services across student affairs could support student mental health needs. These last two volumes, however, are each 10 or more years old. Since their publication, there have been significant changes in the legal landscape, prevalence of certain disorders and conditions, and campus approaches to service provision.

This volume is intended to examine mental health issues for the benefit of practitioners who are not trained and licensed counselors or psychologists—addressing how campuses can be prepared for and respond to these issues. Although some of the chapters address mental illnesses (i.e., specific diagnosed or diagnosable disorders), the broader focus is mental health writ large. For example, several chapters address the adjustment concerns that are commonly faced by some populations of students (such as international or military-connected students) or as the result of situational factors (such as campus crises). In developing this volume, we sought input from senior student affairs professionals about what mental health issues were most concerning or challenging on their campuses. Certainly, there are many issues and populations of students that are not covered within this book. As our society and campuses continuously evolve, there will be endless opportunities for colleagues to follow us in delving into new issues and approaches to addressing and fostering student mental health.

Our goal is to provide a resource for student affairs administrators who are seeking information and guidance on practices regarding emerging issues and challenges related to student mental health. We hope that this book helps readers cultivate a community-centered understanding of and sense of shared responsibility for promoting mental health, supporting those with mental disorders, increasing knowledge about best practices for service provision, and generating strategies for dealing with mental health issues pertaining to specific student populations and issues.

We have organized this book into three sections, reflecting some of the complexities and differences in content knowledge necessary to properly address mental health issues on campus. The first two chapters provide contextual and foundational information related to current student mental health trends. Chapter 1, by Susan Stock and Heidi Levine, opens the book by providing a layperson's overview of some of the more common mental health issues facing students, as well as strategies for effective intervention. In Chapter 2, Ben Locke, Jon Brunner, and David Wallace present overviews of counseling center data regarding student clients and clinical trends, as well as a review of evidence-based practices in the provision of counseling services.

The second section of chapters focus on populations of special interest. We recognize that many groups of students could warrant their own chapters regarding mental health needs, and in this volume, we have chosen three such groups that have received recent attention. In Chapter 3,

Jane Thierfeld Brown, Lisa Meeks, and Michelle Rigler offer a primer on students on the autism spectrum, providing information on students with and without mental health challenges, as well as campus support strategies. Following in Chapter 4, Ted C. Bonar discusses the specific mental health needs of veterans and other military-affiliated students. Last in this section, Chapter 5, by Susan Prieto-Welch, explores the needs and challenges of and for international students.

The third section is composed of chapters that address bigger picture, systemic issues related to mental health faced by colleges and universities. Chapter 6, written by Alan Goodwin, focuses on students "at risk" threats toward self or others and the multiple legal, ethical, and cultural considerations that must be addressed within the campus environment. In Chapter 7, Micky Sharma and Christopher Flynn delineate goals, plans, and intervention strategies related to large-scale campus crises. Daniel Eisenberg, Sarah Ketchen Lipson, and Julie Posselt write about the connections between resilience, retention, and mental health in Chapter 8.

Our volume ends with a chapter by Robert Bonfiglio, long-time senior student affairs officer and leader in student affairs. Bob addresses the future of mental health on campuses by addressing two major forces on campus, which are at times in conflict: working from an ethic of care while attending to tenets of risk management.

We have both had the privilege to work, over the past 30 years, with many gifted colleagues in counseling centers and divisions of student affairs. Our knowledge of the issues presented in this volume is informed by their experience and wisdom. We hope that this book provides readers with some tools they will find useful in meeting the challenges presented by the changing face of student mental health needs and the campus environment.

Heidi Levine
Susan R. Stock
Editors

References

Benton, S. A., & Benton, S. L. (Eds.). (2006). *College student mental health*. Washington, DC: NASPA.

Center for Collegiate Mental Health. (2016, January). *2015 annual report* (Publication No. STA 15–108). University Park, PA: Author.

Kadison, R., & DiGeronimo, T. F. (2005). *College of the overwhelmed: The campus mental health crisis and what to do about it*. San Francisco, CA: Jossey-Bass.

Office of Civil Rights. (2010, December 16). Complaint No. 15-10-2098. [Letter to Spring Arbor University]. Cleveland, OH: U. S. Department of Education, Office for Civil Rights. Retrieved from http://www.bazelon.org/LinkClick.aspx?fileticket=WGmoOxFqnto%3D&tabid=313

Reynolds, A. L. (2008). *Helping college students: Developing essential support skills for student affairs practice.* San Francisco, CA: Jossey-Bass.

HEIDI LEVINE is vice president for student development and planning at Simpson College; she is trained as a counseling psychologist and has prior experience directing college counseling and health services.

SUSAN R. STOCK is the executive director of student health and counseling services at Northeastern Illinois University. She is a counseling psychologist with experience in multiple student affairs departments.

1

This chapter provides an overview of common student mental health issues and approaches for student affairs practitioners who are working with students with mental illness, and ways to support the overall mental health of students on campus.

Common Mental Health Issues

Susan R. Stock, Heidi Levine

In this chapter, we provide an overview of mental health issues commonly found on college and university campuses. Our purpose is not to provide detailed diagnostic criteria (though we describe some of the characteristics found in current diagnostic manuals, such as the *Diagnostic and Statistical Manual of Mental Disorders*, 5th Edition (DSM-5; American Psychiatric Association, 2013)), nor to allow or encourage those who are not licensed counselors or psychologists to diagnose mental disorders. Rather, our aim is to facilitate basic recognition of mental and emotional health issues and offer ideas for interventions and support that can be appropriately offered by staff beyond the counseling center.

Overview of Common Mental Health Disorders

While college students may experience the full range of mental health disorders found in the population at large, we focus on those disorders which most frequently affect students: anxiety, depression, alcohol and other drugs, trauma, and eating disorders. In this section, we describe some of the signs and characteristics of these disorders, particularly looking at how these issues may manifest among students or in a college setting.

Anxiety. In recent years, anxiety has overtaken depressive symptoms as the primary presenting issue at college counseling centers (Center for Collegiate Mental Health [CCMH], 2015) and as a significant issue on university campuses in general (American College Health Association [ACHA], 2014). There has also been a rise in anxiety in the general U.S. population (National Institute of Mental Health [NIMH], 2015). The term "anxiety" can cover a broad range of symptoms, some of which may warrant attention from a professional licensed counselor or psychologist and some not. Of course, all college students (and all people) experience anxiety at some point in their lives. Given the situational demands of university

New Directions for Student Services, no. 156, Winter 2016 © 2016 Wiley Periodicals, Inc.
Published online in Wiley Online Library (wileyonlinelibrary.com) • DOI: 10.1002/ss.20187

campuses—personal, academic, financial, and interpersonal stressors, many of which students may be facing in unique ways for the first time—it is no surprise that anxiety is a common concern.

Anxiety disorders are diagnosed when the worry or fear is so significant to the person that it affects her or his daily functioning, and has continued for a long period of time with the symptoms being present more days than not. Anxiety manifests in many ways. Sometimes the fear is very specific and/or limited to a particular situation. These specific fears are referred to as phobias. Given their limited scope, the fear-inducing stimuli may be relatively avoidable and therefore not significantly or consistently affect daily living. For example, a college student with a phobia of elevators may be able to climb stairs in her residence hall, her classroom buildings, and the gym and therefore avoid the fear-causing stimulus. However, if in the next semester, that same student is assigned to a classroom on the 30th floor of a high-rise building, she may not be able to attend class, which would have a significant impact on her daily experience.

Situational factors define other anxiety disorders as well. Someone with social anxiety disorder, for instance, may be a stellar student and produce excellent solo work, but be hampered in his ability to work on group projects, give oral presentations, and/or chat at networking events. The person with social anxiety disorder experiences overwhelming worry and self-consciousness about everyday social situations. The worry often centers on a fear of being judged by others, or behaving in a way that might cause embarrassment or lead to ridicule.

Panic disorder refers to situations in which feelings of terror occur suddenly and repeatedly, often without warning or an easily identifiable trigger. Sometimes people have panic attacks, which is a single instance of panic as described previously. Having panic attacks frequently and chronically can lead to a diagnosis of panic disorder. The person having a panic attack experiences not only the emotional component of fear but also intense physical symptoms such as sweating, chest pain, a rapid or irregular heartbeat, and/or the feeling that they are choking. It is not unusual for a person experiencing a panic attack to believe that they are having a heart attack.

Lastly, the broadest type of anxiety disorder is called generalized anxiety disorder. This features intense worry and concern regarding many aspects of one's life that does not match a more realistic appraisal of the situation(s). For example, someone with generalized anxiety disorder may find herself unable to stop worrying about school, family, finances, her health, and her school performance, despite the lack of any obvious reason to worry. People with generalized anxiety disorder tend to expect disaster and go about their daily lives anticipating the worst outcomes.

Depression. Following anxiety disorders, depression and other mood disorders are the most frequently occurring mental health issues among the general population and on college campuses. Depression is diagnosed in approximately 7% of the general population and 9% of college-aged adults; much less commonly, bipolar disorder occurs in approximately 2.6% of the population (NIMH, 2015). Responses to the 2014 National College Health Assessment (NCHA) indicate that 33% of participating students felt so depressed that it was difficult to function at least once in the prior year, and 62% reported feeling "very sad" at least once in the past year (ACHA, 2014).

The hallmark sign of depression is a persistently sad or low mood. However, sadness or feeling "depressed" is sometimes a normal response to life events, such as the ending of a relationship or disappointment. Two features that generally differentiate depression from normal sadness or "the blues" are the persistence and pervasiveness of the mood. One of the diagnostic criteria for depression is that this mood has lasted for a period of 2 weeks or longer and that during this time, the person has felt depressed more often than not. It is important to note that some events—particularly grieving the death of a close friend or family member—typically lead to feelings of sadness and loss that extend well beyond this period of time; with grief, however, the grieving person is often able to experience increasingly frequent periods of happiness or other emotions, whereas the depressed person often feels little or no lifting of the depressed mood. For example, students being sad and preoccupied and not feeling like engaging in normal social activities for a few weeks after the break-up of a romantic relationship are likely having a normal response to loss. If, however, students stop attending class and work, spend most of the day in bed, aren't eating or bathing regularly, and are avoiding contact with friends and family, there is a good likelihood that they have slipped into a period of depression.

Sometimes the person experiencing depression does not actually feel sad or down. Anger and irritability are also common emotional signs of depression. And especially in cases of more severe depression, the person may experience a kind of numbness, not really feeling any emotions at all. Part of this emotional numbing frequently includes a lack of ability to enjoy things that had previously been pleasurable. Students experiencing this sign of depression may talk about simply not finding anything fun or meaningful anymore; life just feels kind of flat, as if all the zest had been washed away.

Other signs of depression include difficulties with sleep (such as early morning wakening, excessive sleeping, not feeling rested or refreshed from sleep), change in appetite (sometimes an increase in appetite and eating, but more commonly loss of appetite), loss of motivation and ability to concentrate, social withdrawal and isolation, feelings of hopelessness, and thoughts of death and suicide (Chapter 6 addresses issues related to suicide and self-harm).

Although less commonly occurring, bipolar disorder typically first occurs in early adulthood, often (though not always) following prior periods of depression. Individuals with bipolar disorder fluctuate between states of depression and mania—periods marked by extraordinarily high levels of (often unproductive) activity, expansiveness and exaggeration of mood, and feelings of grandiosity that can lead to impaired judgment and risky behavior. Individuals with mania feel a decreased need for food and sleep, which are subtly different from the loss of appetite or ability to sleep soundly that depressed individuals often experience. As an example, a student who had previously been academically strong and interpersonally outgoing and easy to get along with but who suddenly becomes increasingly belligerent and harassing in their interactions with others, stops doing their academic work but stays up all night writing "creative" pieces that make little sense to readers, and damages others' property may be demonstrating the signs of a manic episode.

Alcohol and Other Drug Use.   Students' use of alcohol (and, to a lesser extent, other drugs) has been a challenge throughout the history of higher education in the United States (Barber, 2011). Most students who use alcohol do so in relatively low-risk social and recreational ways but some slip into misuse, consuming alcohol as a way to cope with stress or manage emotions. At the far end of the spectrum, a small but still attention-worthy number of students develop substance abuse disorders or addictions.

Factors that have contributed to concerns about student alcohol and drug use include the disruptive (and sometimes dangerous) impacts students' misuse of alcohol have on other members of the campus and extended communities and the extent to which alcohol and other drug misuse can be linked to injury and death. According to the 2014 NCHA Survey (ACHA, 2014), two-thirds of participating students at campuses across the United States reported using alcohol at least once in the preceding year. Among those students, 22% reported consuming seven or more drinks in one sitting at least once, and 53% reported experiencing at least one adverse incident (such as injuring themselves, forgetting or regretting something they did) related to their alcohol use. At the worst end of the spectrum, in 2005, approximately 1,825 college students died from alcohol-related accidents (Hingson, Zha, & Weitzman, 2009).

The degree of visibility of alcohol-related incidents on college and university campuses, along with the degree to which U.S. culture has normalized excessive alcohol and drug use among college students (even while decrying the negative impacts of that use), can make it difficult to determine just how prevalent clinically abusive levels of alcohol and drug use actually are. Whether differences are due to effects of being in an environment in which high-risk alcohol use is normative or to a kind of self-fulfilling prophecy that equates college attendance with heavy alcohol use, it can be challenging to separate the student who is experiencing what will prove to be a behavioral anomaly regarding alcohol use from the student who is developing (or already has) a serious substance abuse problem.

Signs that a student may be moving from an abusive use of alcohol or other substance to a substance abuse disorder often involve the frequency with which the student is using the substance; however, some individuals with substance abuse disorders are able to go extended periods without using. Whether the substance use is daily, weekly, or more intermittent, the person's ability to control consumption when using is an important factor in determining the extent of the problem.

As individuals escalate in their abuse of physically (and, to some extent, psychologically) addictive substances, their tolerance typically increases. This means that it takes more of the substance for the individual to feel any effect, and that the individual may not "look" as impaired as someone else using the same amount might. This tolerance and the individual's increasing use in order to achieve even a baseline state are among the diagnostic indicators of a substance abuse disorder.

Frequently, the signs of a substance abuse disorder involve changes and losses in other aspects of the individual's life. The student with a substance abuse disorder may have increasing difficulty meeting academic and other work demands, often declining noticeably in their academic performance. It is very likely that their behavior when under the influence, or other aspects of their use (such as the time and money they spend using), will contribute to conflicts in relationships, often leading to the loss of intimate relationships and friendships with those who do not also use.

Trauma Response.   Psychological trauma, or just "trauma," was long thought of as something that only military combat veterans or those in war-torn countries experience. Although these populations experience trauma, and we have students from both categories on our campuses, in more recent years, trauma has been understood more broadly. It is important to note that students' exposure to trauma, and type of trauma, varies widely depending on the campus and nature of the student body. Sexual assault is one type of trauma that rightfully gets a good deal of attention, but students come to college with a variety of traumatic experiences including reactions to gun violence and police shootings of unarmed African American men.

The American Psychological Association (n.d.) defines trauma as "an emotional response to a terrible event like an accident, rape or natural disaster" (para. 1). A trauma response can be caused by a single incident, something that happened several times, or chronic, ongoing experiences. Additionally, a trauma response may be triggered by a very recent experience or one that happened long ago. Trauma responses can resurface, especially if something happens that feels similar to the time when the initial trauma was inflicted. (See Flynn and Sharma in Chapter 7 for a discussion of the impact of campuswide traumatic events.)

The manifestations of trauma response can vary widely, dependent on the initiating incident, the person, and the resources and support that he or she has had access to, past and present. These reactions can occur immediately after the trauma or appear long afterward and may be relatively short or long-lasting. Shortly after the traumatic experience, shock and denial are common. Longer term reactions may include flashbacks, rapidly fluctuating emotions, avoidance of situations or people that are reminiscent of the initial trauma experience, and difficulty in interpersonal relationships. Many

NEW DIRECTIONS FOR STUDENT SERVICES • DOI: 10.1002/ss

of these responses initially develop to help the person avoid the traumatic situation or things that remind the person of the trauma. For example, it is common for a person who was recently in a car accident to initially avoid the street where the accident occurred. However, if as time goes by, that avoidance generalizes to a fear and avoidance of cars and driving, a strong startle response to any vehicle noise, and anger directed at loved ones who drive to work, then the initial and perhaps healthy and self-protective response has developed into something problematic.

Many college students come to campus with trauma histories, having experienced sexual assault; childhood verbal, physical, or sexual abuse; natural disasters; a car or other accident; and/or violence in their homes or neighborhoods. And similarly, many of our students experience trauma during the time they are our students and that has increased with frequency of violent incidents at everyday venues such as malls and train stations. It is also important to recognize the impact of vicarious trauma. Vicarious trauma refers to trauma that one witnessed or experienced secondhand. Although the reactions of people who directly experience trauma may be different from those of people who experience vicarious trauma, both can have negative impact and are worthy of attention.

Eating Disorders.   Eating and body image issues are frequently found on college and university campuses, although the actual prevalence can be difficult to ascertain. This is for several reasons: First, there is a good deal of shame and stigma regarding the behaviors associated with eating disorders, so it can be assumed that self-report of these behaviors seriously underestimates the prevalence. Second, the assumption that eating and body image issues exist only in certain populations (particularly European-American women) may lead to a lack of assessment and intervention in other populations. Third, current diagnostic criteria lead to eating disorder diagnoses only at fairly severe levels of distress and impairment. This means that those in the less-severe range may not be categorized as having an eating disorder. However, eating and body image issues exist on a continuum, and destructive behavior and/or emotional distress are worthy of attention and intervention, whether or not diagnostic criteria are met.

With the previous caveats regarding prevalence data, one estimate is that in the United States up to 30 million people of all ages and genders suffer from an eating disorder (defined as anorexia nervosa, bulimia nervosa and binge-eating disorder) (Wade, Keski-Rahkonen, & Hudson, 2011). Although these three eating disorders have complex diagnostic criteria, their hallmark symptoms are as follows: Anorexia nervosa features restriction of food intake, a distorted sense of the body in that very thin individuals will see themselves as heavy, and often significant weight loss. Bulimia nervosa typically includes ingestion of large amounts of food, with some type of compensatory behavior, such as vomiting, excessive exercising, or use of medication such as laxatives. People with binge-eating disorder eat large quantities of food but rarely engage in the compensatory behavior. All of these diagnoses include a significant focus on food and concern about body shape and size.

Although these concerns exist throughout the general population, various groups of college students may be particularly vulnerable, either exhibiting current problems or engaging in behavior that may put them at risk. For example, one study found that 91% of women surveyed on a college campus had attempted to control their weight through dieting. Twenty-two percent reported that they dieted "often" or "always" (Shisslak, Crago, & Estes, 1995). Although contrary to cultural stereotypes, some men also experience difficulties with eating and body image (Bulik, 2014). Other groups such as athletes and gay men may also possess certain vulnerabilities that may cause them to be more likely to engage in disordered eating or have a distorted body image.

The very situations that increase the chances of someone having difficulty with eating or body image are reinforced by the broader U.S. culture, which may be reflected in a particular campus culture. This is unique among emotional concerns: one does not see billboards, for instance, touting the benefits of depression. However, college students are bombarded with messages that encourage them to evaluate their bodies negatively and to engage in unhealthy behaviors to change those bodies. For example, having a "lose the most weight" contest at a campus recreation center may reinforce or introduce unhealthy eating habits or a negative body image.

Eating and body image issues can have serious impact on individuals and campus communities. Due to the impact on the physical body, eating disorders have the highest mortality rate of all mental disorders (Sullivan, 1995). Students in the severe ranges of these disorders may need to take time away from campus to regain their mental and physical health, as the impact of the eating disorder can lead to impairment significant enough that the student is unable to function sufficiently to remain a college student. Additionally, eating disorders can have a ripple effect on a residence hall community, specific academic major, student organization, and others, so that the community or communities warrant intervention as well as the individual.

Roles of Nonmental Health Professionals

Although students experiencing a number of the conditions we described clearly would benefit from treatment with mental health professionals, there is still an important role for student affairs professionals to play in working with these students. According to the ACPA/NASPA Professional Competency Area of helping and advising (ACPA/NASPA, 2015), at the most basic level, all student affairs professionals should be able to demonstrate the ability to establish rapport with students, use of active listening skills, facilitation of decision making and goal setting, basic crisis intervention skills, and the ability to make effective referrals. Regardless of whether students seek assistance from mental health professionals, it is important for them to feel cared about and supported by other campus staff. This demonstrates the essential respect that our professional ethics demand (ACPA, 2006), and it conveys to students that there are multiple places where they can find help and can instill hope in cases where students are deeply struggling.

At the same time, student affairs professionals who are not licensed professional counselors or psychologists need to recognize where the limits to their helping roles lie. The extent to which students who are dealing with the kinds of issues presented in this chapter are unable to manage the activities and fulfill the ordinary life expectations of college students indicates the importance of helping that student attain more specialized assistance or treatment. Certainly campus staff can and do continue to have supportive relationships with these students, but setting and maintaining appropriate parameters in those relationships requires not sliding into a quasitherapeutic role.

Strategies and Recommendations

- Learn about mental health. All student affairs professionals should seek opportunities to learn about mental health issues—both common mental illnesses and factors that promote mental health. The more knowledgeable staff are the more successfully conditions that promote all students' well-being can be developed.

- Adopt "gatekeeper" models. Models such as "Question-Persuade-Refer" (QPR) have been developed to assist campuses in creating a safety net for students in distress. These models involve training staff and faculty across the institution to recognize and appropriately respond to students who may be at risk of suicide or other significant problems. These models can be extended to broaden awareness of mental health issues and encourage appropriate help-seeking.

- Maintain community expectations. In some situations, a student's behavior may be sufficiently disruptive or otherwise in violation of community standards to warrant action through a student conduct process. Although this may seem obvious, there are also times when we may feel that it is "kinder" to excuse a student's behavior when we know (or think we know) that a student is experiencing some kind of mental health problem. However, placing the responsibility for the behavior on the student creates the potential for the student to learn from the incident, perhaps including the expectation that the student take steps to better manage the mental health condition.

    ◦ Focusing on and addressing problematic behavior (as opposed to requiring that students engage in some form of treatment), even in the presence of an identified condition or disability, is also within an institution's rights, as long as expectations are consistently enforced.

○ Failing to hold students accountable for their behaviors communicates that we believe they are "too sick" to be held responsible—a message that can either erode their sense of self or, if true, indicates that we should be having different conversations regarding their ability to maintain their student status (see Chapter 6 for more regarding student rights and mandatory withdrawal policies).

• Make appropriate referrals. Effective referrals are built on an accurate understanding of the student's perceptions of their situation, sharing concrete examples of the student's concerning behaviors, and a spirit of respect and trust, along with good knowledge about campus and community resources.

○ Unless the situation is an imminently life- or safety-threatening emergency, referrals should be presented in a manner of openness and offering a suggestion, conveying the understanding that ultimately it is the student's choice of whether they accept the referral.

○ In offering a referral, it is important to convey the message that the referral agent will be helpful and (when possible) that you know and trust that person or agency.

○ It is often helpful to offer to assist in implementing the referral through such steps as providing information about the student and their situation (with the student's permission), or accompanying them when they schedule and/or attend their first appointment.

• Maintain interpersonal boundaries. It is essential to establish clear and appropriate interpersonal boundaries with students in distress.

○ This includes not personally "owning" responsibility for either the student's problem or improvement, recognizing the limits of one's professional expertise, and not getting pulled into a quasitherapeutic role.

○ That last point can be particularly challenging for newer professionals, or when dealing with students who tell you that you are the "only" person with whom they ever felt comfortable talking.

○ Failing to set appropriate limits in these situations can leave the staff person feeling increasingly burnt out or resentful, may keep the student from getting the level of care needed and can ultimately put the staff person and institution at legal risk.

References

ACPA: College Student Educators International & NASPA: Student Affairs Administrators in Higher Education. (2015). *Professional competency areas for student affairs educators*. Washington, DC: ACPA & NASPA.

ACPA: College Student Educators International. (2006). *Statement of ethical principles and standards*. Washington DC: ACPA. Retrieved from http://www.myacpa.org/ethics

American College Health Association. (2014). *National College Health Assessment*. Retrieved from http://www.acha-ncha.org/reports_ACHA-NCHAII.html

American Psychiatric Association. (2013). *Diagnostic and statistical manual of mental disorders* (5th Ed.). Washington, DC: American Psychiatric Association.

American Psychological Association. (n.d.). *Trauma.* Retrieved from http://www.apa.org/topics/trauma/index.aspx

Barber, J. P. (2011). If curbing alcohol abuse on college campuses is an impossible dream, why bother with interventions aimed at curbing abuse? In P. M. Magolda & M. B. Baxter Magolda (Eds.), *Contested issues in student affairs: Diverse perspectives and respectful dialogue.* Sterling, VA: Stylus Publishing.

Bulik, C. (2014). *Eating disorders essentials: Replacing myths with realities.* Presented at the NIMH Alliance for Research Progress Winter Meeting, Rockville, MD.

Center for Collegiate Mental Health. (2015). *2014 annual report* (Publication No. STA 15–30). University Park, PA: Pennsylvania State University.

Hingson, R. W., Zha, W., & Weitzman, E. R. (2009). Magnitude of and rends in alcohol-related mortality and morbidity among U.S. college student ages 18–24: Changes from 1998 to 2005. *Journal of Studies on Alcohol and Drugs* (Suppl. 16), 12–20.

National Institute for Mental Health. (2015). *Anxiety* disorders. Retrieved from http://www.nimh.nih.gov/health/topics/anxiety-disorders/index.shtml

Shisslak, C. M., Crago, M., & Estes, L. S. (1995). The spectrum of eating disturbances. *International Journal of Eating Disorders, 18*(3), 209–219.

Sullivan, P. F. (1995). Mortality in anorexia nervosa. *American Journal of Psychiatry, 152*(7), 1073–1074.

Wade, T. D., Keski-Rahkonen A., & Hudson J. (2011). Epidemiology of eating disorders. In M. Tsuang & M. Tohen (Eds.), *Textbook in psychiatric epidemiology* (3rd ed., pp. 343–360). New York, NY: Wiley.

SUSAN R. STOCK *is executive director of student health and counseling services at Northeastern Illinois University.*

HEIDI LEVINE *is vice president for student development and planning at Simpson College.*

2

This chapter provides a brief overview of the psychological issues facing today's college students, information about students receiving mental health services, and an evidence-based model describing the practice and functions of today's counseling centers.

Emerging Issues and Models in College Mental Health Services

Ben Locke, David Wallace, Jon Brunner

American society remains underresourced in response to the epidemic of mental health issues among its citizens; the human and financial costs weigh heavily on the fabric of our country. It is frequently reported that at least one out of four adults suffers from some form of mental health disorder, and the National Survey on Drug Use and Health (NSDUH; Substance Abuse and Mental Health Services Administration [SAMHSA], 2014) reported that 18.5% of adult Americans (18 and older) experienced mental illness in the past year, with 4.2% having a serious mental illness. The rate of mental illness for young adults (18–25) is even higher at 19.4%. In addition, the NSDUH also reported that 8.5% of American adults had a substance use disorder during the past year.

With close to 70% of high school graduates going on to postsecondary education (Institute of Education Sciences, National Center for Education Statistics, 2015), we would expect college campus populations to reflect the national mental health trends of America's young adults. Serving as a barometer for such pressures, campus counseling centers have been reporting increasing levels of demand and an increase in the number of students with severe mental illness (Gallagher, 2014; Reetz, Krylowicz, & Mistler, 2014; Reetz, Barr, & Krylowicz, 2013). Longitudinal studies indicate that successive generations of college students are demonstrating increasing levels of severe mental illness (Twenge & Campbell, 2009; Twenge et al., 2010). In addition to increased prevalence and severity of mental illness, today's college students also appear to be more willing to seek help for mental health concerns, a trend that may contribute to the increased demand for services on campus. The 2014 Healthy Minds Study (Eisenberg, 2014) found that 98% of students would be willing to accept someone who received mental health treatment as a close friend, and only 15% felt that receiving mental health treatment was a sign of personal failure.

New Directions for Student Services, no. 156, Winter 2016 © 2016 Wiley Periodicals, Inc.
Published online in Wiley Online Library (wileyonlinelibrary.com) • DOI: 10.1002/ss.20188

Table 2.1. Student Report of Distress and Dysfunction

Reported Symptoms	Percentage
Felt overwhelming anxiety	51.0%
Felt things were hopeless	44.8%
Felt overwhelming anger	36.3%
Felt so depressed that it was difficult to function	31.1%
Seriously considered suicide	7.4%
Intentionally cut, burned, bruised, or otherwise injured themselves	6.0%
Were in an emotionally abusive intimate relationship	9.25%

Source: ACHA, 2013; Spring/Fall; N = 202,344

Today's traditionally aged college students are ethnically diverse, lead protected and structured lives, emphasize achievement and accomplishment, are skilled in multitasking, place high value on peer relationships, and have difficulty learning from failure (Levine & Dean, 2012). They show greater acceptance of differences and are both technologically advanced and dependent. They are also defined by the highest levels of stress and anxiety compared to any prior generation (American Psychological Association, 2015; Howe & Strauss, 2000, 2007; Levine & Dean, 2012). Further, in 2014, first-year college students reported the lowest level of emotional health in 25 years (New, 2015).

Further evidence of increasing dysfunction and distress is apparent in self-report survey data from the National Collegiate Health Assessment (NCHA) by the American College Health Association (ACHA, 2013). Forty-five percent of the general population of college students report that some aspect of their lives is traumatic or very difficult to handle. Table 2.1 summarizes additional distressing experiences reported by a surprising number of college students surveyed.

Moreover, the top 10 reasons for poor academic performance reported by students are almost all psychological, as shown in Table 2.2. Psychological reasons that affect academic performance include both individual experiences (depression or stress) and contextual/relational experiences such as concern for another person or relationship difficulties. One large survey (with a 57% response rate) at a Midwestern public university found that one third of students had some form of "mental health problems." Two years later, 60% of the students who originally reported mental health problems still had those problems and less than half had received treatment during the prior 2 years (Zivin, Eisenberg, Gollust, & Golberstein, 2009). Although this was one study at one institution, it highlights the potential unmet need for mental health treatment. Further examining rates of mental illness among college students, Eisenberg (2014) found that rates of depression were stable from 2007 to 2014, at 9 to 10%. This is consistent with NCHA findings that that 9 to 11% of students reported being diagnosed and treated for depression from 2009 to 2013. The same was true for

Table 2.2. Top Issues Affecting Student Academic Performance

Issues	Percentage
Stress	28.25%
Anxiety	19.65%
Sleep difficulties	19.45%
Cold/flu/sore throat	14.1%
Work	13.9%
Depression	13.3%
Internet use/computer games	11.3%
Concern for a troubled friend or family member	10.2%
Relationship difficulty	9.15%
Participation in extracurricular activities (e.g., campus clubs, organizations, and athletics)	9.1%

Source: ACHA, 2013; Spring/Fall; N = 202,344

college students being diagnosed and treated for anxiety, with rates ranging from 10% in 2009 and 2010 to more than 12% from 2011 to 2013 (ACHA, 2013, 2014).

Substance abuse is also a concern on today's campuses. The consequences of binge drinking, including sexual assaults and other violence, remain one of the most intractable problems in higher education. According to the NSDUH report (2014), nearly 60% of students used alcohol and 39% report binge drinking, though binge drinking did decline between 2002 and 2013. The CORE Institute survey (Southern Illinois University CORE Institute, 2013) reports a stable binge-drinking rate of 43% from 2011 to 2013. Further, college students have a higher rate of binge drinking than age-matched peers (National Institute on Alcohol Abuse and Alcoholism, 2015). The NSDUH survey (SAMHSA, 2014) reported that, following alcohol, marijuana is the most frequently used substance and that monthly use is increasing (2002–2013, from 17.3 to 19.1%). This rate has been replicated in other studies (ACHA, 2014; Johnston, O'Malley, Bachman, & Schulenberg, 2013).

As Hunt and Eisenberg (2010) point out, the mental health issues of college students today are of significant concern and present a great challenge for campuses. Because campus counseling centers play a pivotal role in student wellness, it is vital to understand which students are seeking mental health services and how their concerns reflect national mental health trends.

Overview of Counseling Center Clients

The Center for Collegiate Mental Health (CCMH) was established in 2005 for the purpose of accurately describing students receiving mental health services in college counseling centers (Locke, Bieschke, Castonguay, &

Hayes, 2012). CCMH is a membership organization of more than 380 college and university counseling centers that contribute anonymous, standardized data about the students they treat. The most recent CCMH annual report summarized data from 139 college counseling centers describing 100,736 college students in treatment (CCMH, 2016). The standardized "big data" provided by CCMH make it possible to accurately describe the students who seek mental health care in higher education and the nature of their presenting concerns.

Who Seeks Mental Health Treatment. The 2015 CCMH annual report (CCMH, 2016) indicates that students presenting for treatment at counseling centers represent a broad range of students when considering such characteristics as gender identity, sexual orientation, race/ethnicity, international students, first-generation college student, and academic status (see Table 2.3). Use of mental health services tends to parallel institutional enrollment with some general exceptions, such as underuse by men (36.2%) when compared to 60% of female respondents in national surveys (e.g., ACHA, 2014). In contrast to some reports, a nationally representative CCMH study found that racial/ethnic minority students use counseling centers proportionally to their campus populations (Hayes et al., 2011), indicating that minority students in general neither underuse nor overuse mental health services. However, this same study found that racial/ethnic minority clients also tend to present for treatment with significantly higher levels of distress across multiple concerns including depression and anxiety. It is possible that this could be attributed to the sometimes hostile environment experienced by racial/ethnic minority students both in society and on college campuses.

Why Students Seek Mental Health Treatment. In order to examine the question of why students seek treatment, CCMH gathers data about students' presenting concerns via an instrument called the Clinician Index of Client Concerns (CLICC), a list of 43 presenting concerns for which clinicians (a) check all that apply and (b) pick the "top-most" concern of those checked. Both approaches to quantifying presenting concerns are summarized in Table 2.4 and the results are largely similar. "Check-all-that-apply" data indicate how common a given concern is, whereas the "primary concern" indicates how often a concern is the foremost problem. As noted in Table 2.4, anxiety, depression, relationship problems, stress, and family are the top five primary presenting concerns followed by academic performance, interpersonal functioning, grief/loss, mood instability, and adjustment to a new environment. It is worth noting that although self-esteem and sleep did not make the top 10 primary concern list they are among the top 10 "check-all" concerns, which means that they frequently co-occur with many primary concerns. Regarding alcohol and drugs, alcohol is a concern for 10.8% of clients, the top concern for 2%; drug use is a concern for 6.7% and the top concern for 0.9%.

Table 2.3. Counseling Center Client Demographics

What is your gender identity? N = 84,695

Woman	62.6%
Man	36.2%
Transgender	0.3%
Self-Identify	0.8%

Sexual Orientation N = 78,935

Heterosexual	84.7%
Lesbian	1.6%
Gay	2.8%
Bisexual	5.7%
Questioning	2.3%
Self-Identify	3.0%

What is your race/ethnicity? N = 80,039

African-American/ Black	9.2%
American Indian or Alaskan Native	0.4%
Asian American/Asian	6.9%
Hispanic/Latino/a	7.6%
Native Hawaiian or Pacific Islander	0.2%
Multiracial	4.5%
White	69.5%
Self-Identify	1.7%

Are you an international student? N = 80,638

Yes	5.2%
No	94.8%

Are you the first generation in your family to attend college? N = 72,019

Yes	22.5%
No	77.5%

Current academic status: N = 83,113

Freshman/first-year	20.1%
Sophomore	20.4%
Junior	22.4%
Senior	21.4%
Graduate/professional degree student	14.1%
Nonstudent	0.2%
High school student taking college classes	0.0%
Nondegree student	0.3%
Faculty or staff	0.1%
Other	1.0%

Source: CCMH, 2016

These data demonstrate that presenting concerns often overlap and that certain concerns (e.g., sleep or self-esteem) may play a prominent role in student distress. However, these issues may not be identified as the primary focus of treatment when ranked by university counseling center staff. These clinical trends are consistent with general population survey

Table 2.4. Top 10 Presenting Concerns as Determined by CLICC Data

Concern	Check All That Apply (multiple per client)	Primary Concern (one per client)
1.	Anxiety (56.9%)	Anxiety (20.0%)
2.	Stress (46.6%)	Depression (15.8%)
3.	Depression (45.9%)	Relationship problems-specific (9.4%)
4.	Family (31.6%)	Stress (5.9%)
5.	Relationship problems-specific (29.1%)	Family (4.5%)
6.	Academic performance (28.0%)	Academic performance (3.9%)
7.	Interpersonal functioning (23.9%)	Interpersonal functioning (3.8%)
8.	Self-esteem/confidence (22.8%)	Grief/loss (3.6%)
9.	Sleep (15.4%)	Mood instability (2.6%)
10.	Adjustment to new environment (14.0%)	Adjustment to new environment (2.6%)

Source: CCMH, 2016

data in that anxiety and depression are the primary mental health concerns of in both populations. However, though these two concerns are very frequent components of distress, they are not always the most important. For example, university counseling center staff rank anxiety as a concern for 55.1% of clients but identify it as the primary concern for only 19.6%. Similarly, depression is a concern for 46.3% of clients, but it is the top concern for just 15.6%. This differential reflects the fact that many aspects of life contribute to common symptom patterns and each individual's distress (and path to recovery) is unique (CCMH, 2016). Further, although some concerns are much less common (e.g., eating/body image is a top concern for 2.1% and psychotic symptoms is a top concern for 0.2%), these less common concerns are also potentially lethal, are potentially disruptive to the community, and require extensive expertise and time to treat effectively.

A critical mental health concern in higher education is the frequency of suicidal thinking and the risk it represents to students, the community, and institutions. In 2009, CCMH partnered with the NASPA Assessment Consortium to conduct a national survey of college students using CCMH data definitions. Results from over 28,000 students across 42 institutions found that 14% of the general student body reported "seriously considered attempting suicide" in their lifetime and less than 4% reported attempting suicide in their lifetime (CCMH, 2011). The CCMH 2015 annual report concluded that 32.9% of students seeking services on campus reported a lifetime history of "seriously considered attempting suicide" and 9.5% had attempted suicide at some point. In comparison, CLICC data indicate that suicidality is a current concern for 9.5% of clients and is the top current concern for 1.4%. Considered together, these data points make it clear that suicidal thinking is very common lifetime experience for counseling center clients and a current concern for about 1 out of 10 of these students. This underscores previous research indicating that counseling center clients are 18 times more at risk for suicide than the general population and that counseling centers are highly effective at managing this risk (Schwartz, 2006).

Mental Health Histories.   With a better understanding of prevalence (such as frequency of mental health concerns) it is useful to examine prior treatment indicators to understand how the severity (or chronicity) of mental health concerns is changing over time. First, it is important to note that counseling center use has been found to be increasing at five to seven times the average rate of institutional growth over the last 5 years (CCMH, 2016). This means that increased overall enrollment is not responsible for the increased demand for services. According to the 2015 CCMH annual report, 1 out of 2 clients have been in counseling before; 1 out of 3 have taken a psychiatric medication, and roughly 1 in 10 have been psychiatrically hospitalized (CCMH, 2016). These prior treatment trends have been surprisingly stable over the last 5 years despite the dramatic growth in use. Within the general student body prior treatment rates are two to five times lower than counseling center clients: prior counseling (24%), prior medication use (8%), and prior hospitalization (2%) (CCMH, 2011). On one hand, these results confirm hypotheses that counseling center clients are more likely than their peers to have received prior treatment (greater chronicity of concerns). However, the 5-year trend lines for prior treatment indicators among counseling center clients are flat. In other words, despite the dramatic increase in demand, counseling center clients are not reporting increasing levels of prior treatment (i.e., chronicity). If these characteristics are stable, what is changing?

Common Risk Factors Facing Counseling Centers.   Psychiatric hospitalizations are rare and only occur in response to a small number of emergency scenarios, including threat to self, threat to others, or severely impaired functioning. These situations represent extreme risk for students, their community, and the institution. One in 10 counseling center clients has been hospitalized for psychiatric reasons (CCMH, 2016) in comparison to 2% of the general student body (CCMH, 2011). Students who pose a risk to their own safety (suicidality, self-injury, etc.) represent a level of risk that demands a swift and competent response from staff, faculty, peers, and the community—regardless of whether the student truly is at risk or will ultimately follow through with treatment recommendations. The burden of identifying students at risk is felt across the institution, but once identified, these students are typically referred to the counseling center. (See Goodwin, Chapter 6 in this volume, for a more in-depth discussion of at-risk students.)

One of the lesser forms of "threat to self" behavior is nonsuicidal self-injury (NSSI). This often takes the form of cutting but may also include scratching, bruising, burning, or even, in extreme cases, breaking bones. NSSI is disruptive to the residential environment and frequently triggers an institutional response equivalent to a suicide threat. According to the 2015 CCMH annual report, the lifetime prevalence of NSSI has increased slowly but steadily among counseling center clients over the last 5 years, rising each year from 21.8% (2010–2011) to 25.0% (2014–2015). Among the general student body, the lifetime prevalence of NSSI has been reported at 16.0% in the 2009 CCMH/NASPA survey (CCMH, 2011).

Similar to 5-year trend data on NSSI, and in striking contrast to flat trends regarding prior treatment histories, serious suicidal ideation (such as, "I have seriously considered attempting suicide") has risen steadily over the last 5 years, increasing from 23.8% (2010–2011) to 32.9% (2014–2015), a 38% relative increase. Among the general population, this rate is consistently much lower at 14% (CCMH, 2011). Considered together, these 5-year trends represent a persistent growth in "threat to self" characteristics among counseling center clients.

Institutions must be well prepared, trained, and staffed to respond to threat-to-self situations safely and effectively. Indeed, the U.S. Department of Justice made changes to Title II of the Americans with Disabilities Act, which essentially forbid institutions of higher education from removing students from campus for threat-to-self concerns (U.S. Department of Justice, 2010). In a sense, this change can be interpreted as a federal mandate to treat and/or manage threat-to-self concerns within the campus environment. (See Chapter 6 of this volume for a more detailed presentation of these issues.)

The most common presenting concerns among students seeking psychological services are depression and anxiety, with a strong emphasis on relationships and academics, and a broad range of complex and overlapping additional concerns. In addition, 5-year trend data indicate that higher education is facing a new reality of increased demand for mental health services that emphasizes the treatment and management of students with threat-to-self characteristics. As a result of this recent shift, institutions will need to adjust resources accordingly, especially in light of what amounts to a federal mandate to manage at-risk students on campus.

Evolving Models and a Comprehensive Approach

Although counseling remains the primary function, university counseling centers have modified clinical service models over time, often in response to demand exceeding supply. Examples include in-depth initial assessment, brief triage, waitlists, brief therapy models, session limits, and referral to off-campus community providers. These model variations highlight the need for thoughtful administrative decision making, careful and flexible management, and adjustments in funding to meet changing demand.

NEW DIRECTIONS FOR STUDENT SERVICES • DOI: 10.1002/ss

Over time, some counseling centers have merged with health services, and the terms "integrated health care" or "integrative health care" are sometimes used in this context. This model is characterized by medical and counseling staff working within one administrative unit. The ACHA (2010) whitepaper noted that there is no consistent definition of a merged/integrated system, and a 2014 study (Brunner, Wallace, Reymann, Sellers, & McCabe) found that a broad range of clinical practices exist among merged centers. Neither study found evidence to suggest that merged/integrated centers are more effective than counseling and health services administered separately. Regardless of model, collaborative care is vital, and this can be accomplished only through close interprofessional relationships among counseling and medical professionals.

It is increasingly apparent that effective treatment requires more than minimal counseling sessions for some presenting concerns. For example, clinical models that arbitrarily limit sessions without flexibility may be detrimental because students do not fully recover and are subsequently at risk for relapse (LeMoult, Castonguay, Joormann, & McAleavey, 2013).

In addition to strong clinical models, it is important to consider the larger role of counseling centers in education, early intervention, prevention, and resilience building. This more systemic approach was first described in the Cube Model (Morrill, Oetting, & Hurst, 1974), an ecological model that highlighted the multidimensional relationship of the counseling center with all levels of the student experience, from the individual to the institutional. The Global Cube Model (Pace, Stamler, Yarris, & June, 1996) further focused on interactive collaboration among campus partners in meeting student needs.

Other systemic models have emerged more recently, including the campus stakeholder model by the Jed Foundation (2006; Jed Foundation & Education Development Center, Inc., 2011) and public health models (Atkins & Frazier, 2011), which advocate for community education, targeted interventions for those at risk, and support for mental health providers to intervene with those at highest risk.

Effective counseling centers must also join with campus partners to advance mental health initiatives at the level of the institution's strategic plan. Strategies that support resilience, build mental health gatekeeper skills, promote help-seeking, and develop overall well-being can be infused into existing campus classes, learning communities, student organizations, and leadership structures. The leadership of the counseling center, coupled with the skills of involved campus partners, can identify and remove impediments to mental health while strengthening efforts supporting student success and well-being. In this context, a comprehensive counseling center is much more than a mental health clinic; it is engaged in partnerships with students, faculty, and staff across the institution to advance mental health throughout the campus environment.

NEW DIRECTIONS FOR STUDENT SERVICES • DOI: 10.1002/ss

Strategies and Recommendations

• Recognize that demand for mental health services on campus is growing much faster than institutional enrollment (CCMH, 2016) and includes a dramatic increase of students who represent risk to self. Be prepared to explore new funding strategies to meet these trends given the role that counseling centers play in managing risk and facilitating student success.

• The clinical services provide by counseling centers have been found to be as effective as randomized clinical trials for most major mental health concerns (McAleavey, Youn, Xiao, & Castonguay, 2013). In addition, counseling centers have been found to be cost effective and capable of facilitating student's academic success (Eisenberg, Golberstein, & Hunt, 2009).

• Contemporary college and university counseling centers provide a comprehensive range of highly specialized services that benefit the entire university community including clinical services, consultation/collaboration services, prevention/outreach services, and training/education of future mental health providers (Brunner et al., 2014).

• Some mental health concerns (such as anxiety) are common and can be routinely treated by generalists. Other presenting concerns (including psychosis or eating disorders) are rare but require extensive training, expertise, and appropriate resources to manage effectively.

• Recognize and understand the difference between crisis services (rapid access appointments for stabilization and safety planning) and mental health treatment (averaging five counseling appointments). For example, overemphasizing access may lead to a treatment shortage or a lack of time for consultation with faculty and staff.

References

American College Health Association. (2010). *Considerations for integration of counseling and health services on college and university campuses*. Linthicum, MD: Author.

American College Health Association. (2013). *American College Health Association–National College Health Assessment II (ACHA–NCHA II); Reference group executive summary Fall 2013. Reference group data report*. Hanover, MD: Author.

American College Health Association. (2014). *American College Health Association–National College Health Assessment II (ACHA–NCHA II); Reference group executive summary Fall 2014. Reference group data report*. Hanover, MD: Author.

American Psychological Association. (2015, February 4). *Stress in America: Paying with our health*. Retrieved from http://www.apa.org/news/press/releases/stress/2014/stress-report.pdf

Atkins, M. S., & Frazier, S. L. (2011). Expanding the toolkit or changing the paradigm: Are we ready for a public health approach to mental health? *Perspectives on Psychological Science, 6*, 483–487.

Brunner, J. L., Wallace, D. L., Reymann, L. S., Sellers, J-J., & McCabe, A. G. (2014). College counseling today: Contemporary students and how counseling centers meet their needs. *Journal of College Student Psychotherapy, 28*, 257–324.

Center for Collegiate Mental Health. (2011, March). *2010 annual report* (Publication No. STA 11-000). University Park, PA: Pennsylvania State University.

Center for Collegiate Mental Health. (2016, January). *2015 annual report* (Publication No. STA 15–108). University Park, PA: Pennsylvania State University.

Eisenberg, D., Golberstein, E., & Hunt, J. B. (2009). Mental health and academic success in college. *The B. E. Journal of Economic Analysis and Policy*, 9, 1–35. doi: 10.2202/1935-1682.2191

Eisenberg, D. (2014). *College mental health research to practice: Increasing awareness of college students' mental health needs and strengthening the case for resources.* Presented at the meeting of the Association for University and College Counseling Directors, Chicago, IL.

Gallagher, R. P. (2014). *National survey of college counseling 2014* (Monograph Series Number 9V). International Association of Counseling Services. Retrieved from http://www.collegecounseling.org/wp-content/uploads/NCCCS2014_v2.pdf

Hayes, J., Youn, S., Castonguay, L., Locke, B., McAleavey, A., Nordberg, S. (2011). Rates and predictors of counseling center use among college students of color. *Journal of College Counseling*, 14, 105–116.

Howe, N., & Strauss, W. (2000). *Millennials rising: The next great generation.* New York, NY: Vintage Books.

Howe, N., & Strauss, W. (2007). *Millennials go to college* (2nd ed.). Great Falls, VA: Life Course Associates.

Hunt, J., & Eisenberg, D. (2010). Mental health problems and help-seeking behavior among college students. *Journal of Adolescent Health*, 46(1), 3–10.

Institute of Education Sciences, National Center for Education Statistics. (2015). *Immediate college enrollment rate.* Retrieved from http://nces.ed.gov/programs/coe/indicator_cpa.asp

Jed Foundation. (2006). *Framework for developing institutional protocols for the acutely distressed or suicidal college student.* New York, NY: The Jed Foundation.

Jed Foundation & Education Development Center, Inc. (2011). *A guide to campus mental health action planning.* New York, NY: Jed Foundation Campus MHAP and Waltham, MA: Education Development Center.

Johnston, L. D., O'Malley, P. M., Bachman, J. G., & Schulenberg, J. E. (2013). *Monitoring the future: National results on adolescent drug use. Overview of key findings, 2012.* Ann Arbor: Institute for Social Research, University of Michigan.

LeMoult, J., Castonguay, L. G., Joormann, J., & McAleavey, A. (2013). *Depression.* New York, NY: Guilford Press.

Levine, A., & Dean, D. R. (2012). *Generation on a tightrope: A portrait of today's college students.* San Francisco, CA: Jossey-Bass.

Locke, B. D., Bieschke, K. J., Castonguay, L. G., & Hayes, J. A. (2012). The Center for Collegiate Mental Health: Studying college student mental health through an innovative research infrastructure that brings science and practice together. *Harvard Review of Psychiatry*, 20(4), 233–245. doi: http://dx.doi.org/10.3109/10673229.2012.712837.

McAleavey, A. A., Youn, S., Xiao, H., & Castonguay, L. G. (2013, October). *Evaluating routine practice and evaluating the methods of evaluation: How effective are routine practices for different symptom types, and what can different methods tell us?* Paper presented as part of a panel at the conference of the North American Society for Psychotherapy Research (NASPR), Memphis, TN.

Morrill, W., Oetting, E., & Hurst, J. (1974). Dimensions of counselor functioning. *Personnel and Guidance Journal*, 53, 354–359.

National Institute on Alcohol Abuse and Alcoholism. (2015, March). *Alcohol facts and statistics.* Retrieved from https://www.niaaa.nih.gov/alcohol-health/overview-alcohol-consumption/alcohol-facts-and-statistics

New, J. (2015, February 5). Incoming students' "emotional health" at all-time low, survey says. *Inside Higher Education*. Retrieved from https://www.insidehighered.com/news/2015/02/05/incoming-students-emotional-health-all-time-low-survey-says

Pace, D., Stamler, V., Yarris, E., & June, L. (1996). Rounding out the cube: Evolution to a global model for counseling centers. *Journal of Counseling and Development, 74*, 321–325.

Reetz, D., Barr, V., & Krylowicz, B. (2013). The Association for University and College Counseling Center Directors annual survey. Retrieved from http://files.cmc global.com/AUCCCD_Monograph_Public_2013.pdf

Reetz, D., Krylowicz, B., & Mistler, B. (2014). *The Association for University and College Counseling Center Directors annual survey*. Retrieved from https://taucccd.memberclicks.net/assets/documents/2014%20aucccd%20monograph%20-%20public%20pdf.pdf

Schwartz, A. J. (2006). College student suicide in the United States: 1990–1991 through 2003–2004. *Journal of American College Health, 54*(6), 341–352.

Southern Illinois University CORE Institute. (2013). *2011–13 national results executive summary. CORE alcohol and drug survey long form*. Carbondale, IL: Author. Retrieved from http://core.siu.edu/results/index.html

Substance Abuse and Mental Health Services Administration, Center for Behavioral Health Statistics and Quality. (2014). *The NSDUH report: Substance use and mental health estimates from the 2013 National Survey on Drug Use and Health: Overview of findings*. Rockville, MD: Author.

Twenge, J. M., & Campbell, W. K. (2009). *The narcissism epidemic: Living in the age of entitlement*. New York, NY: Free Press.

Twenge, J. M., Gentile, B., DeWall, C. N., Ma, D. S., Lacefield, K., & Schurtz, D. R. (2010). Birth cohort increases in psychopathology among young Americans, 1938–2007: A cross-temporal meta-analysis of the MMPI. *Clinical Psychology Review, 30*, 145–154.

U.S. Department of Justice, Civil Rights Division. (2010). Final rule: Nondiscrimination on the basis of disability in state and local government services. *Federal Register, 75*(178), 56164–56236. Retrieved from http://www.gpo.gov/fdsys/pkg/FR-2010-09-15/html/2010-21821.htm

Zivin, K., Eisenberg, D., Gollust, S., & Golberstein, E. (2009). Persistence of mental health problems and needs in a college student population. *Journal of Affective Disorders, 117*(3), 180–185.

BEN LOCKE *is the senior director of clinical services at Penn State's Center for Counseling and Psychological Services and is also the founder and executive director of the Center for Collegiate Mental Health.*

DAVID WALLACE *is the director of the Counseling Center at the University of Missouri.*

JON BRUNNER *is the executive director of Counseling and Health Services at Florida Gulf Coast University.*

3

This chapter introduces the reader to the autism spectrum and discusses the characteristics, traits, common concerns, and potential supports for this population. The chapter also provides some recommendations for proactive and collaborative support efforts for students with both an autism spectrum disorder and mental health issues.

Mental Health Concerns of Students on the Autism Spectrum

Jane Thierfeld Brown, Lisa Meeks, Michelle Rigler

Autism Spectrum Disorder (ASD) is a complex neurobiological disorder characterized by deficits in communication and social relationships and by restricted, repetitive behaviors. It is defined as a spectrum disorder to highlight the range of symptoms and severity that occur within the diagnosis. To be diagnosed with ASD, an individual must display the following: (a) persistent deficits in social communication and social interaction, and (b) restricted and repetitive behaviors, interests, and activities specified by the level of support needed (American Psychiatric Association, 2013).

ASD occurs across all racial, ethnic, and social groups and its effects last a lifetime. Today about 1 in 68 individuals is diagnosed as being on the autism spectrum (Centers for Disease Control [CDC], n.d.). When compared to previous CDC statistics (1 in 110 in 2006 and 1 in 150 in 2000), the increase in prevalence is evident. Students on the autism spectrum represent one of the fastest growing populations of students on campus (CDC, n.d.). Student affairs professionals are sure to interact with students on the autism spectrum and therefore should take steps to educate themselves and their staff about how to best support and engage with this unique and valuable population of learners.

Characteristics and Traits of Students with Autism Spectrum Disorder

Students on the autism spectrum experience difficulty with executive functioning, which is an impactful issue during the transition to college. Executive functioning regulates the management of everyday life and is a

NEW DIRECTIONS FOR STUDENT SERVICES, no. 156, Winter 2016 © 2016 Wiley Periodicals, Inc.
Published online in Wiley Online Library (wileyonlinelibrary.com) • DOI: 10.1002/ss.20189

known deficit in individuals on the autism spectrum. Cognitive processes such as initiating tasks, prioritizing steps, managing emotions, motivation, time management, and task completion are all part of executive functioning. Many students on the spectrum use their support system as an external "brain." In other words, someone else acts as their executive functioning, managing their everyday life, helping organize them, and reminding them about deadlines. As these students move to the postsecondary environment, deficits in executive functioning may become a source of stress. When deadlines are forgotten, papers are lost, and appointments are missed, students can become frustrated and at risk for failure.

Mental Health and ASD

Many students with ASD will present with concurrent mental health issues; however, ASD itself is classified as a neurobiological disorder, *not* a psychological one. In this case, ASD arrives in advance of the mental health issues. Indeed, it appears that most of the mental health issues that co-occur with ASD result from the social and communication deficits of the disorder. Although mental health diagnoses are secondary in ASD they may be equally, if not more, debilitating. In a 2015 study by Russell and colleagues, the prevalence of anxiety disorders, particularly obsessive-compulsive disorder (OCD), was significantly higher in adults with ASD than in the general population. Russell's findings confirm previous reports (Kreiser & White, 2015; Maddox & White, 2015) suggesting that secondary mental health issues, primarily anxiety disorders, OCD, depression, and attention-deficit/hyperactivity disorder, are common in adults with ASD. Given this prevalence, students with ASD will likely benefit from existing campus mental health services.

Appropriate mental health services can be crucial to students' success both in and outside of the classroom (Meeks, Masterson, Rigler, & Quinn, 2016). For college students with ASD, the stress of the university experience may result in sensory overload, emotional outbursts, and other difficult behaviors related to their autism. These behaviors may appear or are interpreted to be signs of mental illness. Student affairs professionals can help reduce potential exacerbation of symptoms by providing training to the greater community about the positive and challenging aspects of individuals with ASD, along with tips for how to best support this population. Proactive supports work best with students on the autism spectrum. Offices should coordinate efforts, for example, hosting a collaborative support group led by staff from the counseling offices, disability service offices, residence life, and career services. By coordinating efforts, offices can reduce overlap and effectively use institutional resources while providing students with more complete and coordinated support.

NEW DIRECTIONS FOR STUDENT SERVICES • DOI: 10.1002/ss

Common Concerns: Challenges Facing Students with Autism

Many students on the spectrum will never seek or need services on our campuses. Given the opportunity to study an area of interest, coupled with freedom to sleep, eat, play, and work on their own, these students will thrive and many times excel. For this population, the academic rigors and intellectual challenge of college are stimulating. Some students, however, will arrive unequipped to handle the lack of structure and layers of social nuance that drive campus culture. Student affairs professionals can assist students by better understanding common triggers and reactions in the ASD population.

Stress Management.   Students with ASD often misinterpret their symptoms of stress for illness and respond by going to health services or staying in bed until they "feel better." To better understand the impact of stress, students with ASD need to be taught in a concrete way what stress feels like. The identification of the signs of stress can begin by presenting the various domains and impacts of stress so students can make a connection to what they are feeling. Some of these symptoms fall in domains including cognitive (loss of memory, lack of concentration, insomnia, and self-doubt), emotional (irritability, moodiness, loneliness, depressed state, and short temper), behavioral (fidgety, pacing, change in sleep pattern, change in eating habits, aggression, and withdrawal), and physical (racing heart, headache, muscle tension, digestive issues, dry mouth, and exhaustion).

Once students with ASD are able to better identify how stress feels, they can begin to identify what triggers stress and do the important work of developing a plan to manage that stress before it creates other difficulties. It is imperative that students with ASD understand that their response to stress must be managed appropriately to avoid having a negative impact on others around them or other difficulties that could result in a code of conduct violation, suspension, expulsion, or legal intervention.

Student Conduct.   The behavior of an individual on the spectrum can result in a referral to counseling or report to a disciplinary team (e.g., behavioral intervention team and students of concern committee). Behavior leading to such a referral might include self-stimulation or "stimming," the act of providing self-stimulation in the effort to focus. Potentially troublesome or misinterpreted behaviors include pacing, head banging, rocking; audible verbalization of thought (external self-talk); talking about inappropriate subject matter (e.g., bombs or guns); perceived stalking (not picking up on social cues that someone does not want to be bothered); poor hygiene; and failure to attend class or eat meals.

These behaviors can be alarming to a student affairs professional unfamiliar with ASD. Moreover, these behaviors can be mistaken for signs of serious psychological disorders. It is important to distinguish ASD-related behaviors from the onset of serious mental health concerns. For example, the first signs of a mood disorder or psychosis often occur in young adulthood, a time that aligns with beginning a college career. It is critical that student affairs personnel and counseling staff recognize and distinguish between a student with ASD performing self-stimulation, displaying self-talk to mitigate anxiety or recall social rules, for example, and a student having a psychotic episode. It is also important for student affairs officials to avoid making assumptions about a student's threat to self or others based on perceived concern about a student with ASD. And in situations involving student conduct processes, all decisions should be based on the student's actual behavior, as opposed to predictions based on the student being on the ASD spectrum.

Social Skill Deficits.   Unwritten social contracts for behavior often escape the student on the spectrum. For this reason, most individuals on the spectrum require very direct instruction around social and relationship rules (Meeks et al., 2016). To be able to understand the nuances of social interactions, potential situations need to be dissected and analyzed with the student. Then support personnel can help the student develop a response that mitigates the impact of any social gaffe.

A strategy that can be employed to help students with ASD engage in typical social situations is the creation of social scripts. Social scripts are intended to help students with ASD prepare for typical social interactions. These could include conversation starters, questions, and potential responses to questions within conversations. By developing a script and practicing it, students with ASD may be able to engage in conversations with peers without the stress they often feel in social situations. This strategy is helpful in developing social confidence and can encourage students with ASD to engage in conversations with peers.

Student Affairs Offices: Sources of Support

Students on the autism spectrum, just like neurotypical students, interact with all Student Affairs areas. It is essential that Student Affairs practitioners be knowledgeable about the ways they can effectively engage with and support students with ASD.

Disability Services.   The disability services offices are responsible for ensuring equal access to qualified students with disabilities. They determine whether or not a student meets the criteria for receiving accommodations as a student with a disability and, if so, which accommodations are reasonable in the various educational contexts. Disability services staff are not all equally knowledgeable about ASD. This, coupled with the fact that students with autism are less likely than students with other disabilities to disclose and seek services, can result in disparate support across campuses.

The ability of the disability services provider to proactively work with students on the autism spectrum is central to a successful experience. When students do not disclose or seek support at the beginning of college, there is a risk that their needs will not be addressed until they are in trouble, academically or behaviorally (Masterson & Meeks, 2014). Failure to disclose the disability often necessitates faculty and staff making decisions and accommodations on the fly.

Students on the spectrum often require some typical accommodations like extended time on tests, separate rooms for tests, note takers for lectures, and possibly a single room in the residence halls (this will be addressed further under the section on residential life). However, many students on the spectrum also require additional, nontraditional supports to fully engage in college. For example, an extension of the number of counseling appointments afforded to the general population (perhaps 15 versus 10), or assistive technology that aids in getting the students' thoughts into writing (Meeks & Geither, 2014) could be helpful to a student with ASD.

For students on the spectrum with mental health issues, nontraditional accommodations may be even more important. For example, extra time may not be beneficial for an exam when a student needs to stim. Instead, the ability to walk or pace while completing an exam may prove a more effective accommodation for a student on the spectrum.

Disability service providers must be careful to consider the impact of ASD on the individual student. Given that previous behavior is the best indicator of future behavior, a detailed intake should take place and should include a frank discussion about prior issues, possible hospitalizations, and times away from school. This discussion should be student led, allowing the student to disclose and solve problems at their comfort level. A discussion of this nature might include such questions as, "Tell me about a time you became overwhelmed, how you handled it, how could you have improved your reaction, and how can we reduce the likelihood of this occurring?" The discussion should also include the student's wishes should things go awry. For example, the disabilities services provider might inquire about how the student prefers to be counseled or assisted if things are going well. Students are the experts on their past and disabilities and should direct the supports, communicating their needs to the provider.

Finally, disclosure is often a large point of contention for students on the spectrum. Some students prefer to disclose directly to their faculty whereas others (and we highly recommend this approach) disclose via the disability services office, which provides standardized policies and procedures for accommodation requests, approvals, and notifications. Additionally, working through the disabilities office ensures that students are protected under the Americans with Disabilities Act (ADA), the federal laws that safeguard equal access to higher education. Disclosures via disability services also often include proactive advice for faculty about interacting with students on the spectrum and encouragement for faculty to contact the office if they have any questions or concerns.

Counseling Centers.   Similarly to the disability services office, the counseling center works with students to try to build coping techniques to address their psychological symptoms and increase overall functioning.

These might include developing executive functioning skills such as time management, planning, and attention; learning methods to reduce anxiety; mindfulness and meditation training; and building an understanding of one's triggers while increasing self-awareness so that students understand if and when they need assistance and how to use their support system. To help students recognize what anxiety feels like, some professionals use biofeedback. Biofeedback allows students with autism to visualize their physiological symptoms associated with specific feelings (e.g., high blood pressure, heart rate, and pulse) through various pictures or technical representations projected on a computer screen. The students learn to use techniques to reduce the anxiety and are able to view reductions in physical symptoms and gain to control these functions.

Students can also use counseling as a way to increase self-advocacy skills. For students on the spectrum, learning to communicate their needs while framing their strengths and abilities is vital to long-term success in college and adult life. Students with ASD and mental health issues may require interventions that vary from the typical talk therapy available on college campuses. Some students prefer cognitive behavioral therapy whereas others respond well to ASD support groups that focus on social skill development and anxiety reduction. It is important for counselors to understand the mental health issues that co-occur with ASD and have expertise in this population or have the ability to refer to counselors with ASD expertise off campus.

Career Services.   Employment is an essential part of developing self-efficacy (Gerhardt & Lainer, 2011). Stable employment is also positively associated with subsequent reductions in clinical symptoms and maladaptive behaviors (Bissonette, 2013). Newman and colleagues (2011) estimate that 50–70% of individuals on the spectrum are unemployed, with even more individuals receiving insufficient benefits and compensation that is unequal to that of their peers. Unfortunately, obtaining a college degree does not necessarily translate to improved employment outcomes for individuals with ASD (Howlin, 2000). A recent study found that 58% of young adults on the autism spectrum are unemployed (Roux et al., 2015). These statistics highlight the growing need for support services that capitalize on the strengths of individuals with ASD while fostering career development (Meeks, Masterson, & Westlake, 2015).

Although there have been many improvements over the past decade with respect to special education and multidisciplinary treatment interventions, postsecondary transitions to employment for individuals with ASD remain fraught with challenges (Meeks, Masterson, & Westlake, 2015). Career services specifically play a critical role in preparing students with ASD for the world of work. Internships and work experience are crucial to most students but even more important for students with ASD who also have mental health issues (Bissonette, 2013; Rigler, Rutherford, & Quinn, 2015). Although these are important experiences, they often also cause an increase in stress as students learn a new set of social rules, new schedule, and new routines.

These students require repetition and rehearsals to learn appropriate behaviors for an employment setting, which can be accomplished through role-playing and supervised work, internship, and volunteer experiences (Geller & Greenberg, 2010; Meeks et al., 2015). A job coach or peer mentor may be an appropriate support for students learning workplace etiquette. As well, specialized multimodal support programs, like Career Connect (Meeks et al., 2015), provides coordinated supports to students engaging in employment recruitment programs specifically targeted toward individuals with disabilities. In these models, support offices provide services in a coordinated fashion with the goal of helping students with disabilities, and ASD particularly, gain access to employment opportunities.

Finally, students with ASD need to learn how the academic accommodations they receive at school translate to the workplace and how to advocate for themselves. Without a comprehensive method of providing support to these students, they risk missing the workplace skills necessary to successfully transition and the world misses out on the opportunity to engage with a highly creative and intelligent group of individuals.

Residence Life.   Students on the spectrum with mental health issues often experience difficulties in the residence halls. Students who struggle with anxiety and depression may have difficulty living in such an intensely social environment and begin to decompensate (e.g., stop attending class and lack proper hygiene). To proactively mitigate these situations, student affairs personnel may consider accommodating students with ASD with a single room. A single room, when available, provides students with the ability to control their sensory sensitivities, meditate, and stim in a private environment. Private space also ensures that other sensory issues can be privately addressed. Lighting, noise, and temperature can all be sources of stress in a shared environment. Putting the control for the aforementioned items in the hands of the student with ASD reduces stress and any roommate issues that result from disparate personal needs and preferences.

Given the importance of this accommodation to the overall success of the first-year student, every effort should be made to provide a single room where that accommodation has been recommended, without assigning all students with ASD into a specific residence hall. In the absence of single rooms, institutions should strongly consider a release from first-year housing requirements for those students with ASD and co-occurring mental health issues. Many families find that a multistep transition (that includes living at home the first year) provides more structure and less stress for the student.

Furniture items may also help reduce stress. Many students with ASD purchase beanbag chairs that envelop the student while sitting. As well, hanging hammock chairs are a wonderful source of positive pressure as they "hug" the user. These chairs also rock, providing the student on the

New Directions for Student Services • DOI: 10.1002/ss

spectrum with two sources of appropriate stimulation: swinging (rocking) and positive pressure—both provide enough sensory feedback to calm the nervous system. Similarly, a rocking chair can provide comfort to the student who is unable to secure the hammock chair (due to residence hall regulations). Most important, these items are not outside of the norm for a college residence hall. In fact, many college students have similar chairs or purchase them after seeing their peers'.

Training the residence life staff on approaching and addressing issues that involve students on the spectrum is paramount. It is important that residence life staff differentiate behaviors related to ASD from more serious mental health conditions. Although ASD and mental health conditions can coexist, if normative ASD idiosyncrasies are mistaken for serious mental health concerns, the result is often further isolation and stigmatization of the student. Indeed, understanding the characteristics of ASD can make the difference between identifying inappropriate behavior/social deficits and correcting it versus escalating a rather benign behavioral quirk.

Other Student Affairs Programs.   Student affairs personnel can provide additional support by being mindful of the needs of individuals with ASD when planning activities and services. As one example, a separate "low sensory zone" area for studying or socializing could be created to encourage students on the spectrum to engage in student affairs programs without the fear of becoming over-stimulated. Another way to assist students on the spectrum more broadly is to put policies, procedures, forms, and other essential items online and in a straightforward and easily accessible manner. Language should be clear and free of ambiguity.

Specialized or low-sensory orientations are another mechanism for supporting this population. Many students on the spectrum simply forgo orientation—a critical part of understanding the new environment and the rules—due to overstimulation. By offering an alternative orientation or "low stimulation" alternate activities you can create a more inclusive and welcoming transition to the school or program.

For many years, families had very few options for their college-aged children on the autism spectrum. Students who were bright and capable but symptomatic could not assimilate to college living or function on the average college campus. Through improved treatment, early intervention, greater supports in K–12 and increases in supports in the college setting collectively changed access to higher education for this population. Students on the spectrum are coming to college and represent some of the most creative and intelligent minds of our time. With appropriate support and accommodations, students on autism spectrum (including those with mental health issues) now have options for postsecondary education. Student affairs professionals can help support students through their roles and help the community understand and embrace the diversity and value individuals with autism bring to our campuses.

Strategies and Recommendations

- Provide staff training. Student affairs offices need training for their staff and for the faculty. They can also refer individuals to helpful videos designed for faculty, like the video prepared by the Organization for Autism Research (2011).
- Students on the spectrum are students first. Disability never excuses behavior and conduct codes should be consistently enforced.
- Consult your disability offices on all accommodations. Faculty or other student affairs staff do not have the authority to decide the accommodations a student may need.
- Offer additional support. Services such as social skill groups, executive functioning support, coaching, and peer mentors can be particularly helpful to students with ASD and depression or anxiety. These programs may include weekly individual support, sensory integration, and specialized first-year experience classes.
- Seek expertise. Your campus may need assistance to develop strategies that work with your campus culture. Having professionals on campus with advanced training can allow your institution to work effectively with students with ASD.
- Know your limits. Know your professional and personal limits and refer students for more in-depth assistance when appropriate.
- Use a universal design philosophy on your campus. There are many students who would benefit from a less stressful environment on campus, low-key social options, and structured social activities. Provide these along with thoughtful sensory spaces (swings, meditation spots) and mindfulness sessions. These suggestions will assist in the mental health of all students, especially those on the autism spectrum.

References

American Psychiatric Association. (2013). *Diagnostic and statistical manual of mental disorders* (5th ed.). Washington, DC: Author.

Bissonette, B. (2013). *The complete guide to getting a job for people with Asperger's syndrome*. London and Philadelphia, PA: Jessica Kingsley Publishing.

Centers for Disease Control and Prevention. (n.d.). Data and statistics. Retrieved from http://www.cdc.gov/ncbddd/autism/data.html

Geller, L., & Greenberg, M. (2010). Managing the transition process from high school to college and beyond: Challenges for individuals, families, and society. *Social Work in Mental Health, 8*(1), 92–116.

Gerhardt, P. F., & Lainer, I. (2011). Addressing the needs of adolescents and adults with autism: A crisis on the horizon. *Journal of Contemporary Psychotherapy, 41*(1), 37. doi:10.1007/s10879-010-9160-2

Howlin, P. (2000). Outcome in adult life for more able individuals with autism or Asperger syndrome. *Autism: The International Journal of Research and Practice, 4*(1), 63.

Kreiser, N. L., & White, S. W. (2015). ASD traits and co-occurring psychopathology: The moderating role of gender. *Journal of Autism and Developmental Disorders, 45*(12), 3932–3938.

Maddox, B. B., & White, S. W. (2015). Comorbid social anxiety disorder in adults with Autism Spectrum Disorder. *Journal of Autism and Developmental Disorders, 45*(12), 3949–3960.

Masterson, T., & Meeks, L. (2014). What support might help students with autism at university. *Good Autism Practice, 15*(1), 47–53.

Meeks, L., & Geither, E. (2014). Writing and the autism spectrum: Helping students through the process. *Good Autism Practice, 15*(2), 79–83.

Meeks, L., Masterson, T., Rigler, M., & Quinn, E. (2016). *Parties, dorms and social norms: A crash course in safe living for young adults on the autism spectrum.* London: Jessica Kingsley Publishers.

Meeks, L., & Masterson, T., & Westlake, G. (2015). Career Connect: A collaborative employment resource model for serving students with ASD in higher education. *Career Planning and Adult Development Journal, 31*(4), 25–35.

Newman, L., Wagner, M., Knokey, A.-M., Marder, C., Nagle, K., Shaver, D., ...Schwarting, M. (2011). *The post-high school outcomes of young adults with disabilities up to 8 years after high school. A report from the National Longitudinal Transition Study-2 (NLTS2)* (NCSER 2011–3005). Menlo Park, CA: SRI International. Retrieved from www.nlts2.org/reports/

Organization for Autism Research. (2011). Understanding Asperger syndrome: A professor's guide [Video file]. Retrieved from www.researchautism.org/resources/AspergerDVDSeries.asp

Rigler, M., Rutherford, A., & Quinn, E.(2015). *Developing identity, strengths and self-perception for young adults with Autism Spectrum Disorder: The BASIC College Curriculum.* London: Jessica Kingsley Publishers.

Roux, A. M., Shattuck, P. T., Rast, J. E., Rava, J. A., & Anderson, K. (2015). *A national autism indicators report: Transition into young adulthood.* Philadelphia, PA: Life Course Outcomes Research Progra, A.J. Drexel Autism Institute, Drexel University. Retrieved from http://drexel.edu/autisminstitute/research-projects/research/ResearchProgramin LifeCourseOutcomes/indicatorsreport/#sthash.31XId4lN.0dNgPmmN.dpuf

Russell, A. J., Murphy, C. M., Wilson, E., Gillan, N., Brown, C., Robertson, D. M., McAlonan, G. M. (2015). The mental health of individuals referred for assessment of autism spectrum disorder in adulthood: A clinic report. *Autism.* doi: 10.1177/1362361315604271

JANE THIERFELD BROWN *is assistant clinical professor at Yale University, Yale Child Study, Director of College Autism Spectrum, and former director of student services at the University of Connecticut Law School.*

LISA MEEKS *is an assistant professor of medicine at the University of California, San Francisco School of Medicine and director of medical student disability services.*

MICHELLE RIGLER *is director of disability services at the University of Tennessee-Chattanooga (UT-C) and founder and program director of MOSAIC, a specialized program for students on the spectrum at UT-C.*

NEW DIRECTIONS FOR STUDENT SERVICES • DOI: 10.1002/ss

4

This chapter provides an overview of common challenges faced by military-connected students on university campuses. The characteristics, culture, and experiences of service members and veterans are described through vignettes based on military-connected students.

Mental Health and Military-Connected Students on Campus: Culture, Challenges, and Success

Ted C. Bonar

Universities, colleges, and their communities require understanding of the culture, needs, strengths, skills, and vulnerabilities of service members, veterans, and all partners and families of these students. As of 2013 in the United States, approximately 1 million students in postsecondary institutions were engaged with current or previous active duty, National Guard, or Reserve military service, and 96% of all higher education institutions nationwide enrolled these individuals. Since 2001, over 5 million service members and veterans have pursued higher education (Cate, 2014; Queen & Lewis, 2014; U.S. Department of Veterans Affairs [USVA], 2014). Students such as these, as well as their partners and/or family members, are commonly referred to as military-connected students in order to address this distinct population in higher education.

Institutions struggle to determine consistent and reliable ways to quantify the population of military-connected students on their specific campuses, and often cannot easily discern veteran status from that of active duty, National Guard, reserve personnel, or their dependents (Molina, 2015). Therefore, a campus may find it challenging to support the mental health and wellness of this population. This affects the military-connected individual's day-to-day life, available programs and resources, institutional awareness of the different needs of military-connected students, and the overall environment and campus culture that intersects with the unique background of these individuals. This chapter provides an overview of various aspects of experiences of veteran and military-connected students to inform campus administrators and student affairs professionals how to better support the overall mental health and well-being of this population.

NEW DIRECTIONS FOR STUDENT SERVICES, no. 156, Winter 2016 © 2016 Wiley Periodicals, Inc.
Published online in Wiley Online Library (wileyonlinelibrary.com) • DOI: 10.1002/ss.20190

The Military-Connected Student, Campus Culture, and Resources

Data regarding the gender, age, race, socioeconomic status (SES) background, marital status, and dependents of military-connected individuals in the United States are easily accessible (Molina, 2014; U.S. Census Bureau, 2015; U.S. Department of Defense [USDoD], 2015a). Other elements of individual identity, such as sexual orientation, political affiliation, gender identity, religion, or spiritual identification, may be more difficult to quantify but must be considered as part of the military-connected student's experience. A common description of the military-connected student given by campus personnel might be, for example, an athletic, Caucasian male with short hair who is older than the average student. Although this is not inherently incorrect, it is insufficient, and captures neither the diversity of the individual, the group as a whole, nor the experiences carried by the students.

Although active military service members are approximately 85% male (USDoD, 2015a), only 75% of student veterans are male (USVA, 2014). It is expected that the number of women veterans in both the general population and on campus will continue to rise (National Center for Veterans Analysis and Statistics, 2011). Some military-connected students are not veterans: they may be active duty and attending school part time, or they may serve in the National Guard or reserves and share many of the same experiences of both traditionally aged college students and active duty personnel (Cate, 2014). Although these students balance vastly different military and student cultures, they may not use available campus programming and services as they do not yet identify as veterans, and they have nonnegotiable responsibilities to the military, preventing them from participation in traditional student programming.

In 2015, 59% of active duty, National Guard, or reserve service members concurrently enrolled as college students reported that their institutions met their current needs. For veterans, only 42% agreed that their institutions met their needs (Queen & Lewis, 2014). Universities and colleges have long had specific campus programs and resources for veterans. Financial aid departments often include GI Bill points of contact and can be a primary link for veterans; 79% of institutions report having a dedicated staff member or office specifically to assist veterans with financial education benefits (Queen & Lewis, 2014). Between 2009 and 2012, universities dramatically expanded their military- and veteran-focused resources and programming, and in 2012, 71% of reporting campuses indicated that they intended to provide services to service members and veterans as a part of their long-term strategic plan (McBain, Kim, Cook, & Snead, 2012). Programs on campus can include veteran student organizations, veteran service offices, specific veteran-specialty outreach and counseling programming, dedicated resident life placement, dedicated military-based curriculum, and other student affairs professionals with oversight of campus-specific military and veteran operations.

This is a start, but insufficient. Although institutions regularly offer assistance with financial aid and 63% offer information to prospective students about service member and veteran programing at job fairs (with 32% participating in promotions on military bases), only 21% of institutions offer customized student orientation programming for veterans, 14% offer some form of formal mentoring or advising program run by faculty veterans or staff veterans, and 22% have specialized mental health counseling (Queen & Lewis, 2014). Specific efforts to address veterans' needs inherently address some needs but not others, and efforts to increase awareness, programming, and resources must continue.

On-campus veterans' centers have become commonplace. Over 70% of the 690 institutions that enroll veterans surveyed by the American Council on Education in 2012 had such a center (McBain et al., 2012). But there are often veterans who have little or no interest in connecting with other veterans. And, again, not all military-connected students are veterans. It is insufficient to rely on one support office as the sole resource or focal point for campus awareness. Campus initiatives to train institution personnel as mentors, allies, peers, or culturally competent in any specific cultural area must be matched equally with initiatives designed to address the unique experience of the military-connected student on campus.

Diversity, Culture, and Experience

Although specific support offices such as cultural centers or LGBTQ (lesbian, gay, bisexual, trans, queer) offices (as examples) are imperative components of the campus experience, no single office serves the needs of veterans at an institution, including veterans' centers. Focusing on a single cultural identifier, including veteran status, may miss the essential nature of a person and the concern at hand. Further, female veterans tend to use veterans' centers less frequently than their male counterparts, rendering these resources less useful for female veterans seeking support or peer connection (DiRamio, Jarvis, Iverson, Seher, & Anderson, 2015). Female veterans often have different needs than male veterans, and it is important that a campus be able to respond to the specific needs of female veterans as opposed to relying on a one-size-fits-all approach to military-connected students (Iverson, 2011).

Military-connected students often experience multiple conflicting messages, both self- and community-driven: the identity of "I am a veteran" or "I am military" may correspond poorly with "I am a student." A campus community may claim "military friendly" status, but that campus may in fact have limited resources for military-connected students. Diversity training for students and faculty may omit any discussion of veterans or military connection, thereby leaving many on the campus vulnerable to cultural missteps. On-campus cultural competency training of students, faculty, and staff would enlighten many to the concerns that follow.

Several vignettes follow intended to describe the depth and breadth of the military-connected student's experience and potential challenges on campus. The fictionalized vignettes (based upon real-life individuals) highlight common experiences that are noted at the outset. Potential campus resources are considered throughout. It is important to note that campus programming, environment, institution size, and community resources are all highly varied depending on any particular institution.

Jake.   A 29-year-old, undergraduate, single, Japanese-American male of multiracial, ethnic, and national heritage, Jake was a 10-year Marine veteran with three combat deployments. He finished his service as a platoon sergeant and secured a position at the university as a resident advisor (RA); he stated, "I'm a good leader of young men." He sought services at the university counseling center after a conflict with a fellow RA, a 19-year-old gay male. He and Jake argued during a staff meeting, and they each struggled to interact respectfully with the other.

Jake did not express hostility toward his fellow RA based on his identity as a gay man. Jake acknowledged and expressed a lack of understanding and a desire to befriend this individual. Further, although his life was replete with profound, violent trauma (heavy combat experiences and a childhood of a physically violent household), Jake struggled to perform his responsibilities as an RA due less to his trauma history than to the dramatic change of environment and culture. To Jake, traumatic experiences were commonplace, and he repeatedly expressed and displayed resilience, as well as a determination to live by his Marine Corps values of "Honor, Courage, Commitment." The military-connected student's 10-year experience in a culture that overlaps poorly with a campus-based experience heavily influenced each interaction between this former Marine platoon sergeant, his fellow RA, and the first-year university residents in their charge.

Orientation to campus culture for the military-connected individual may be as important as financial or academic advising for Jake. With proper preparation, faculty, staff, and students can be prepared to assist in the negotiation of the cultural gaps between today's young college student and the student with 10 years of military experience. Orientation for RA staff in particular may need to include issues of diversity regarding military culture in addition to other areas of culture. Whereas the veteran carries responsibility to assimilate to the university community, the university also carries responsibility to provide adequate support and orientation for the nonveteran student and staff.

Lyn.   As a 26-year-old undergraduate in 2014, Lyn claimed the following identities: soldier, combat veteran, woman, partnered, lesbian, multiracial, older-undergraduate student, and a desire to be seen as "not military." Lyn served as an Army soldier from 2009 to 2012, and she deployed to Afghanistan in a combat role in 2011. Lyn regularly indicated that her identities were fluid and frequently misunderstood by campus professionals. When she mentioned struggling with general feelings of isolation or academic challenges, she became frustrated by people telling her to "go to the Vet Center" or "visit the LGBTQ support office."

Lyn indicated greater need of special academic and career advising than to connect with veteran or LGBTQ community support. She did not deny the importance of those aspects of her life but did not indicate a struggle to (or even a strong desire) to better connect with these communities. Her more significant struggle was one of "I was a soldier, but now I'm an out-of-place student. I don't know what to do with my life. What should I study?" Although she would have access to academic and career advising services at virtually any campus center, the ability of these centers to address the specific, nontraditional, military-connected student must be encouraged and developed further.

Administration and Policy

There is a need for increased awareness and policies for military-connected students throughout different departments. Military-connected housing is becoming more available at institutions, and has been identified by military-connected students as potentially aiding transitions to campus (McBain et al., 2012). Course credit for military service time is common, but veterans are not always aware of this and may not ask or apply for credit. Institutions themselves may not be able to administratively capture those who may qualify, despite the presence of a veteran-certifying official. Institutions, admissions, and registrars each bear a portion of this responsibility.

Luke.   Luke, a 24-year-old Navy veteran, had slipped through an administrative crack. Luke was a first-year undergraduate after serving 5 years' active duty as an electrician on a submarine. Because he was not aware of the possibility of receiving college credit for his service, he lived in a first-year residence hall along with 18- and 19-year-old students per university policy and was also prohibited from having a car because of first-year restrictions.

When Luke attended a veterans' social event, he spoke about feeling isolated and out of place in the residence hall and frustrated by the car restriction. He questioned whether or not he should stay in school. Luke greatly needed the interactions with fellow veterans, and his participation in the veterans' center and peer-to-peer programming was ultimately crucial to his decision to remain at the university. However, his experience reveals how well-intended programming (such as the housing and parking restrictions) can become misapplied through simple accident, leaving the military-connected student vulnerable to cultural, community, and experiential isolation.

NEW DIRECTIONS FOR STUDENT SERVICES • DOI: 10.1002/ss

Dependents, Reserve, and National Guard

Dependents of military-connected students are less often part of campus discussion, but 44% of student veterans are married and 52% have dependents. Some dependents may also be students (Molina, 2014). Some students may be children of service members or veterans, and should also be considered military-connected.

Military-connected students concurrently enrolled in both school and service, such as students who are in the National Guard or reserve, often experience campus challenges different from veterans. National Guard or reserve members may mobilize unexpectedly during the school year, causing great difficulty in balancing academic, social, and service commitments due to unpredictable and sometimes extended travel. Many experience extended commutes or the financial burden of supporting a family. Some will face a decision of whether to stay in school or drop out following an absence or due to financial responsibilities. National Guard and reserve personnel often speak of feeling socially disconnected from veterans and traditional students alike.

Institutions may consider the need to expand their programming to better integrate nonveteran military-connected students, such as National Guard, reserve, active duty, and dependents of individuals in service. Gender-specific programming at veterans' centers, support groups for military parents, female-specific social networks, coursework sections for veterans only, and on-campus childcare resources have also been identified by veterans as scarce but important factors for military-connected student success (DiRamio et al., 2015; Iverson, 2011)

Dana.   A 20-year-old, partnered, Caucasian, heterosexual, politically conservative Christian female, Dana was a mature, high-achieving student. Her father was a 20-year Army veteran who was stationed in approximately seven different states prior to Dana's entry to campus. As an undergraduate junior, she was engaged to an active duty sailor stationed approximately 800 miles from her campus. Dana's fiancé would be at sea for several months at a time, and she described feelings of isolation and frustration. Dana felt her 20-year-old peers did not understand her stressors, acknowledgment from faculty and staff was difficult to attain, and social connection with other military-connected students such as veterans was unlikely if not impossible.

Shellie.   Shellie entered the National Guard at 17 years old while still in high school. During her first year of college, her unit mobilized for 3 weeks midsemester to respond to the devastation following a hurricane. At 18, Shellie was exposed to long hours, devastated homes, and dead bodies. She then returned to school to resume her academic schedule. Shellie requested academic assistance and accommodations in order to maintain her status during her first semester at school. Shellie deployed with her activated guard unit to Afghanistan for 9 months following her junior year.

NEW DIRECTIONS FOR STUDENT SERVICES • DOI: 10.1002/ss

When she returned to campus after missing a full academic year, she felt alone and isolated, as her friends had graduated and moved away. She felt connected with neither students ("They don't understand," "They ask me if I killed people," "People don't even know what the Guard is") nor veterans ("I don't fit in at the vet center," "I'm not a veteran," "I only see my Guard unit once a month when I leave school for drill"). The diversity of the military-connected student must be better understood in order to ensure that students, such as Dana and Shellie, are able to be successfully retained.

Mental Health Issues

Service members and veterans may experience increased rates of depression, anxiety, posttraumatic stress disorder, sexual assault, suicidal ideation and behavior, relationship concerns, and academic difficulties in comparison to the general population (American Psychological Association, 2015). Military-connected students tend to underuse counseling services in comparison to other identifiable groups on campus (Center for Collegiate Mental Health, 2014). A campus must hold two truths simultaneously: Military-connected students as a group experience a greater risk and higher rates of mental health problems, and yet most military-connected students do not experience clinically significant mental health problems.

Military-connected students are often subject to the expectation by others that their concerns are necessarily military related. Although mental health problems must be rightly understood within a person's culture and context, military connection is but one facet of a person's experience. Some common challenges, such as mood concerns, relationship difficulties, family death, and breakups or divorce, are similar for military-connected and traditional students alike. Military connection may add context but may not be the source of challenges.

Jack.   Jack's first request of the counseling center focused on significant, nonmilitary-related concerns. A 28-year-old, divorced, Caucasian male undergraduate, Jack attended counseling to address his mood and overall stress 1 year after his mother died from cancer. He had experienced a romantic breakup following the death of his mother. He sought counseling services for support as he prepared to graduate and apply to medical school. A Marine right out of high school and for the following 6 years, he married at age 19 and divorced at 21. He participated in heavy combat and saw several dead bodies. However, he did not indicate a lasting concern regarding Posttraumatic Stress Disorder (PTSD). He stated, "I knew what might happen. It was hard, but I was prepared for it." At 27, after the death of his mother, he experienced another romantic breakup and subsequently "felt like a failure." He stated, "Marines are able to figure things out . . . it's what we do. But I can't get this right."

Jack's story belies some common ideas regarding the mental health concerns of veterans on campus: A rugged, combat-decorated Marine with multiple experiences in an environment of death and violence, he required no special accommodations, specific veteran services, advocacy, trauma therapy, or multicultural programming. Rather, he needed the ability to understand and experience the loss of his mother and to include how the military culture and credo had influenced him.

Military Sexual Trauma (MST) and Nonmilitary Sexual Assault. Reported rates of military sexual trauma (MST) vary in prevalence and reliability (USDoD, 2015b). For the individual, specific rates are less important than the environment and circumstances in which it occurs. MST occurs, most often, within a unit or with a known person or group (Morral, Gore, & Schell, 2015). Within military units, one is asked to protect and be protected by all other members of the unit—this is part of military culture.

MST is therefore underreported, as reporting often leads to feelings of banishment, betrayal, and perceptions that the reporter has "broken" the unit due to likely investigations of unit members, which would jeopardize unit cohesion for both the individual who reports MST and the individuals who may be investigated. Even in situations in which reports are made, some of these reports are not investigated at the request of the reporter. Feelings of unit or cultural betrayal can be as profoundly injurious as any initial incident. It is beyond the scope of this chapter to adequately explore these implications and concerns, but it is imperative for campus personnel to be aware of the military-specific dilemmas faced by an individual who has experienced MST.

Megan. Megan was a 27-year-old Army veteran with two deployments to Afghanistan and a third-year undergraduate. She reported having been sexually assaulted by a civilian contractor on base during deployment. In the early-morning hours when Megan was isolated on base, the individual aggressively advanced toward Megan as he was disrobing and yelling in a foreign language, compelling Megan to raise her firearm in self-defense. The incident ended without physical assault or Megan firing her weapon. Megan was left shaken, questioning her safety, training, and protection on base. She reported the incident to her commanding officers, who responded with laughter and the dismissal of the report. Megan was in need of specific trauma counseling with a professional who understood the full context of the life-threatening situation, the betrayal of the reporting process, and the questions of identity Megan then experienced following the incident: "Was I a good soldier?" "I was ready to kill a man. Over this?" "I shouldn't have been there in the first place." "The military betrayed me and I am a bad soldier."

Jill. Jill's story is complex, but one with a clear, important message for campus communities. A 26-year-old, single, Caucasian female undergraduate, Jill was an Air Force veteran with no deployment history. She reported having been sexually harassed in the military, but not sexually assaulted.

NEW DIRECTIONS FOR STUDENT SERVICES • DOI: 10.1002/ss

Upon her first year at her university after separation from the military, she was repeatedly, violently raped by her then-partner. She sought services as a veteran at the local VA hospital for depression, suicidal ideation, and PTSD. Because of the wait time and lack of resources at the VA, she was unable to secure timely mental health care. She then sought services as a student at the university counseling center to address her acute distress, including ongoing, high-risk suicidal ideation related to PTSD. Jill was in need of advanced, evidence-based, short-term treatment for suicidal behavior and PTSD to address a sexual assault and its aftermath that occurred outside of the military community.

Combat Trauma. Individuals who experience military-related or combat trauma can often manage distress and symptoms while remaining in the military: the structure, mission, and shared experience of the military often enable an individual to cope with and move past short-term challenges. However, upon returning to campus life, the distress of PTSD can become overwhelming.

Doug. A second-year undergraduate following 3 years in the Marines, Doug deployed to Afghanistan at age 19 and was involved in several combat missions. On campus as a 23-year-old student, he had nightmares, poor class attendance, depression, suicidal thoughts, and several other symptoms consistent with PTSD. One incident haunted him: he and his unit had to "clear" a building, and he found the dismembered body of a child that had been killed by a grenade he had thrown up a stairway as part of the mission. Doug received evidence-based treatment for PTSD on campus at the counseling center. Rather than becoming resentful at an institution that might refer him to other providers or organizations ("pass me on" or "not deal with me"), he expressed gratitude and loyalty to the institution that provided effective, relevant on-campus treatment. His success as a student was secured and his risk of suicide and other distressing behaviors was significantly reduced.

Reintegration

A common thread in every mental health problem and vignette included in this chapter is the challenge for military-connected students to integrate or reintegrate with campus communities. Sometimes the challenge is cultural (dress, language, and expectations of others), sometimes social (difficulty in finding others of the same type), sometimes identity (military vs. student), and sometimes behavioral (are behaviors symptoms of mental health problems or are they evidence of misapplied military skills). The challenges of reintegration and all concerns mentioned go far beyond what is possible to explore within this chapter, yet these challenges are evident throughout. The nuances of each vignette offer examples and insight into the challenge of integration and reintegration from military to campus member/student.

NEW DIRECTIONS FOR STUDENT SERVICES • DOI: 10.1002/ss

Strategies and Recommendations

- Identify a GI Bill point of contact within financial aid.
- Ensure that an on-campus veteran support office has dedicated space, staff, and resources.
- Establish an active veteran student organization.
- Develop, update, and actively contribute to institutional websites and social media for military-connected concerns.
- Identify processes and points of contact for all military-connected student concerns at each academic, student affairs, housing, financial aid, dean of students, career development, student employment, admissions, registrar, or other relevant department.
- Implement ongoing, self-sustaining cultural training programs to integrate mentors, allies, peers, faculty, and staff in matters related to military-connected students.
- Offer military-specific housing opportunities for military-connected individuals. Implement regularly recurring cultural and mental health training for all medical and clinical counseling staff.
- Initiate and sustain comprehensive orientation efforts for all military-connected students.
- Incorporate specific programming and training curriculum regarding reserve, National Guard, and dependents/partners/families into all aspects of military-connected students.
- Address the need for female-specific social networks within the military-connected community.
- Commit resources toward advanced clinical training for counseling staff to use evidence-based treatment of PTSD as well as suicidal behavior.

References

American Psychological Association. (2015). *The mental health needs of veterans, service members, and their families.* Washington, DC: Author.

Cate, C. (2014). *Million records project.* Washington, DC: Student Veterans of America.

Center for Collegiate Mental Health. (2014). *2014 annual report.* University Park, PA: Pennsylvania State University.

DiRamio, D., Jarvis, K., Iverson, S., Seher, C., & Anderson, R. (2015). Out from the shadows: Female student veterans and help-seeking. *College Student Journal, 49*(1), 49–68.

Iverson, S. (2011). Help female student-veterans feel connected on campus. *Student affairs today: Best Practices and Strategies for Student Affairs Professionals, 14*(8), 1–3.

McBain, L., Kim, Y., Cook, B., & Snead, K. (2012). *Soldier to student II: Assessing campus programs for veterans and service members.* Washington, DC: American Council on Education.

Molina, D. (2014). *Higher ed spotlight: Undergraduate student veterans.* Washington, DC: American Council on Education.

Molina, D. M. (2015). *Military-connected undergraduates: The current state of research and future work.* Washington, DC: American Council on Education.

Morral, A., Gore, K., & Schell, T. (2015). *Sexual assault and sexual harassment in the U.S. Military: Vol 2, Estimates for Department of Defense service members from the 2014 RAND Military Workplace Study.* Santa Monica, CA: RAND Corporation.

National Center for Veterans Analysis and Statistics. (2011). *America's Women's Veterans: Military Service History and VA Benefit Utilization Statistics.* Washington, DC: Department of Veterans Affairs.

Queen, B., & Lewis, L. (2014). *Services and support programs for military service members and veterans at postsecondary institutions, 2012–2013.* Washington, DC: U.S. Department of Education, National Center for Education Statistics.

U.S. Census Bureau. (2015). *Veterans.* Retrieved from www.census.gov/topics/population/veterans.html

U.S. Department of Defense. (2015a). *2013 demographics: Profile of the military community.* Washington, DC: Author.

U.S. Department of Defense. (2015b). *Department of Defense annual report on sexual assault in the military: Fiscal year 2014.* Washington, DC: Author.

U.S. Department of Veterans Affairs. (2014). *Characteristics of student veterans.* Retrieved from http://www.mentalhealth.va.gov/studentveteran/docs/ed_todaysStudentVets.html

TED C. BONAR *is a clinical psychologist based in Columbus, Ohio. He is the executive director of the Campus Readiness Project and has presented and trained at over 100 universities and national conferences on matters related to military service members and veterans' concerns.*

NEW DIRECTIONS FOR STUDENT SERVICES • DOI: 10.1002/ss

5

This chapter describes the mental health status of international students in institutions of higher education, unique challenges these students face and their impact on mental health, and suggestions for ways to address these challenges.

International Student Mental Health

Susan L. Prieto-Welch

In recent years, there has been a shift toward global movement, as seen in increases in tourism and commuting, improvements in ease of communication across the globe, and the global marketplace. In an effort to actively participate in the global marketplace, institutions of higher education in the United States have made concerted efforts to attract international students. One of the main strategic goals for many educational institutions is to recruit these students for "academic, educational and cultural purposes" (Sümer, Poyrazli, & Grahame, 2008, p. 429). International students' presence at U.S. colleges and universities provides opportunities for education and exposure to various countries and cultures for U.S. domestic students, enhancing domestic students' knowledge of international history and issues, as well as helping them develop marketable skills related to diversity and cross-cultural competencies. In addition, upon graduation, international students take with them increased knowledge about the United States and American culture, as well as technical knowledge and skills.

According to the Open Doors Report (Institute of International Education [IIE], 2014), the United States hosted 886,052 international students in 2013–2014, an increase of 8% from the previous year. The presence of these students is economically important. In 2013–2014, they accounted for more than $27 billion in the national economy (IIE, 2014). Despite this significant presence and impact on our country, international students as a group have been one of the most underserved groups of students on our campuses (Mori, 2000).

International students, individuals who leave their home countries in search of opportunities for an education and degree in a different country (Jung, Hecht, & Wadsworth, 2007), often face similar stressors and developmental challenges as domestic students upon entering college or university. These stressors include anxiety related to the unknown and new experiences in the college or university setting, academic pressures, financial

New Directions for Student Services, no. 156, Winter 2016 © 2016 Wiley Periodicals, Inc.
Published online in Wiley Online Library (wileyonlinelibrary.com) • DOI: 10.1002/ss.20191

concerns, concerns related to relationships, and feelings of isolation (Bradley, 2000). These pressures can contribute to the development of mental health concerns for any student, domestic or international. International students have additional unique pressures and struggles, which may interact with and compound the expected pressures just described.

In considering issues relevant to international students, the context in which we understand these issues must be highlighted. That is, international students come to the United States and to the specific community of the institution in which they've enrolled. They must perform in and adjust to a cultural, social, and political context that predates their arrival. It is paramount that we acknowledge and be mindful of existing issues of racism, discrimination, and microaggressions that we see in our country overall and in the specific local and institutional communities to which we belong. Recurring political themes and conversations around immigration and concerns about terrorism are but two examples of issues that can be heated in our country and communities. The existence and impact of these conversations shape and inform international students' lived experience in our communities and affect their adjustment on our campus. It is incumbent upon us, as individuals and institutions, to address any prejudice, discrimination, and microaggressions we might see on our campuses; understand our roles in preventing and/or promoting the negative effects these can have; and institute ways in which we continuously educate ourselves and our own communities while welcoming the international students we invite to our campuses.

Another note regarding context: This chapter is written from the perspective of an author who works with international students at an institution in the United States, and whose experience in college and graduate school was that of an international student. This particular set of lenses informs this discussion of international students and their experiences on U.S. campuses. As we look at our own as well as our institutions' contributions to the experiences of international students, readers are invited to consider their own contexts and perspectives related to working with international students.

Acculturation and Other Stressors

Rosenthal, Russell, and Thomson (2006) surveyed international students at a large university, curious about these students' experiences of their physical and mental health. They report that, in general, most of the students who participated in the survey indicated a positive sense of physical and psychological well-being. This highlights that, in many instances, individuals who journey to a country and culture other than their own for educational purposes report that they are functioning well overall. With this as backdrop, this chapter considers issues and themes specific to international students' adjustment and functioning.

NEW DIRECTIONS FOR STUDENT SERVICES • DOI: 10.1002/ss

Unique sources of stress and struggle for international students include the language barrier faced as many come to a country to study in a language that is not their native tongue (Mori, 2000; Poyrazli, Kavanaugh, Baker, & Al-Timimi, 2004). These authors also note that lower proficiency in English is associated with higher acculturative stress. Unfamiliarity with the American educational system, often quite different from the system in which they grew up and excelled, is another source of struggle, as is the loss of familiar social support networks and the need to establish new ones upon arrival, resulting in feelings of isolation, loneliness, and homesickness (Guidry Lacina, 2002; Olivas & Li, 2006; Mori, 2000; Tidwell & Hanassab, 2007). Cultural misunderstandings, racial discrimination, and cultural isolation may add to their struggles (Yakunina, Weigold, & McCarthy, 2011). These additional layers of pressure and struggle can add to students' experience of stress and difficulties with adjustment, which may lead to mental health concerns (Jung et al., 2007), shown to be related to disruptions in academic functioning and achievement.

The process of adjustment for international students includes acculturation. There are a number of definitions of acculturation; in essence, it is a process by which an individual's behavior, values, beliefs, and cultural identity change as a result of coming in contact with others from a different culture (Lui, 2014; Zhang & Goodson, 2010). Inherent in this process is consideration of the majority or host culture, specifically the existing climate around those who are different (culturally, ethnically, and racially). The more the host culture struggles with being open and welcoming, be it unintentionally or intentionally, the more likely the individual will experience instances of prejudice, racism, and discrimination. These instances, not surprisingly, affect the individual and inform their experience of living in that particular culture and community. As previously mentioned, it is this interaction between the newcomer and the existing environment that is important in understanding any struggles, temporary or more long-standing, that may emerge.

One of the unique dimensions to acculturation for international students is the fact that international students are often quite aware that their tenure in the United States is temporary (Lee & Ciftci, 2013; Misra & Castillo, 2004). As such, these students are sojourners (Mori, 2000), a group in transition for the express purpose of successfully obtaining an education (Guidry Lacina, 2002). They need to balance adjusting to a new culture with maintaining a strong sense of cultural identity with regard to their home culture, as they will be returning after their relatively brief stay in the United States.

Symptoms of adjustment stress can manifest as physical complaints for which there is no physical basis; cognitive fatigue, seen as cultural confusion and disorientation and/or difficulty concentrating; and psychological symptoms including feelings of isolation, sadness, loss, homesickness, resentment, and frustration. These may escalate to feelings of hopelessness and helplessness sometimes associated with depression (Mori, 2000).

Various studies illustrate that similarity between host culture and culture of origin may lessen acculturative or adjustment stress. For example, Yeh and Inose (2003) found that European students studying in the United States reported significantly less acculturative stress than did Asian, African, and Latin American students. Sumer and colleagues (2008) note that the adjustment process becomes more difficult as differences between two cultures increase. Research shows that students from collectivistic cultural orientations coming to the United States show lower levels of adaptation, more dissatisfaction, and higher levels of anxiety than do students from more individualistic societies (Sümer et al., 2008). Students from collectivistic cultures whose values are most discrepant with those represented in U.S. majority culture also happen to be the largest groups of international students—those from Asia. Students from China, India, and South Korea together account for 50% of international students in the United States (IIE, 2014).

Hamamura and Laird (2014) note that East Asian students often have more psychological difficulties than do domestic students, associated with challenges in the process of acculturation. They report increased risk of depression because of language barriers, problems adjusting, lack of social supports and friendships, and lack of familiarity with systems and structures as important contributors to difficulties noted. These researchers note that for East Asian students in particular, an additional source of stress may be high, internalized, and at times unrealistic expectations and a felt sense of pressure coming from family and others at home. Educational achievement and attainment are also important values in these cultures; thus failure or low performance is not seen as an option.

Fundamentally, collectivist cultures value the self in relationship, meaning that individuals see themselves in terms of similarities to and connections with others. Cooperation is highly valued. Behavior is guided by relationships, and the norms, obligations, and duties that go along with them. For example, obedience, conformity, and reliability are prized (Lee & Ciftci, 2013), as is filial piety. The group (or family) is more important than the individual in many respects, and a person's feelings, behavior, and choices may be guided by this value of interdependence. As Liu (2009) states, "The Chinese self is fundamentally a social one" (p. 73).

The values just described are different from those of the United States' individualistic core. In the majority culture in the United States, independence is highly valued, as are competition, autonomy, privacy, and individuation. An individual's personal needs and rights inform decisions and behavior, and assertiveness is desired. For students from Asian countries and cultures, and for those from other parts of the world with strong collectivistic cultures (such as Africa and Latin America), the discrepancy between collectivistic and individualistic values may be strongly felt as they struggle to reconcile both, which may contribute to and perhaps intensify adjustment-related stress.

International students with less or poor social support may be more sensitive to stress and experience higher levels of distress (Poyrazli et al., 2004). Results of the process of acculturation can be associated with a variety of mental health outcomes, particularly if the international student does not have a good support system in place. Liu (2009) notes that the quality of social support can have a direct and buffering effect on stress felt by international students.

In addition to limited social support networks and acculturation adjustment stressors, a number of international students experience much pressure to succeed academically. Trying to do so in an unfamiliar academic system and in a non-native tongue is an additional set of stressors. For a subset of international students, there is a unique, more nuanced dimension to felt pressure to perform academically. Some students are sent to the United States (by their government or another entity) to study in a specific area or field, funded to do so, and are then expected to return home for a career in that particular area. The process of education in the United States can introduce them to other fields and possibilities. This can result in a sense of conflict and impasse, as they have been sent to achieve very clear, unchanging educational and career goals. The combination of these challenges, and attempting to address them in an environment that is unfamiliar in many respects, and perhaps unwelcoming in some ways, may be expressed as symptoms of anxiety and/or depression.

When looking at international students' psychological adjustment, it is helpful to look specifically at stress and coping. One common finding is that international students who interact more with Americans as well as adhere to their host culture show better adjustment (Zhang & Goodson, 2010). It may be that in this process, both sets of students learn about each other and develop more realistic beliefs about each other and each other's cultures. Additionally, the more international students engage with Americans and U.S. culture, the better their language skills, the more they understand the customs, and the more they learn about communication patterns and social interactions in the United States. This can lead to improved self-confidence and feelings of mastery, as well as more connection and less social isolation.

One specific example of this can be found in Zhang and Goodson's (2010) study, which indicated that the more the Chinese students in the study interacted with and adhered to the U.S. culture, the more connected and less socially isolated they felt, which in turn mediated levels of depression. They also found that Chinese students who simultaneously rejected their home culture and had little to do with Americans had the highest depression levels of all the samples. These students had few connections and were thus more isolated.

That said, it is also the case that strong identification with one's home ethnic group may be protective (Iwamoto & Liu, 2010). For some students, affiliation with others from one's home culture, who are more likely to share values, beliefs, and customs, may decrease social isolation and provide social support, particularly in the initial stages of adjustment. This can be helpful in institutions that have a relatively large population of students from a particular country. However, there are instances in which there are few students from one's home country, and the student needs alternate sources of support. Ultimately, a balance between support from others who share cultural beliefs and values, and connections with those from the host culture, is most beneficial.

Considerations for Counseling Centers

Literature on mental health indicates that, as a group, international students are less likely to seek help in the way it is often offered in the United States. Research indicates that international students' usage rates of counseling center services are lower than that of domestic students (Masuda et al., 2009). In some cultures, therapy as we know it is not available; there are other helping networks that an individual might turn to instead, networks that may well be unavailable in the United States. Also, in some cultures helping networks are more informal, and the "how" of help-seeking is most important in order to minimize shame and save face for oneself and/or one's family and community.

International students' concept of mental health itself may be different, and there may be stigma that poses a barrier to help-seeking. Language differences and low language proficiency may be another barrier to help-seeking, as can cultural differences between mental health professionals and the international student. By the time these students seek help, symptoms may have developed and intensified.

Research indicates that 32% of college students endorse symptoms consistent with a mental health diagnosis (Nordberg, Hayes, McAleavey, Castonguay, & Locke, 2013). According to this study, about two thirds of students with significant symptoms do not receive services for the symptoms endorsed. This is seen in the general student population, despite the fact that majority culture values in the United States are reflected in the process of therapy, including a focus on individuals expressing their feelings, asserting their rights, and making their needs known. The potential conflict between values embodied in therapy and an international student's cultural values may pose an additional barrier to treatment-seeking for this student population. These therapeutic assumptions may pose conflicts for the international student, who may not access help as early on in their process of struggle and, when they do, may prematurely drop out of treatment (Guidry Lacina, 2002). An example of contrasting values exists in the Chinese culture, where emotional restraint is important, as is harmony in relationships (Liu, 2009). The individual will not make a demand on others or try to change their external environment to meet their individual needs. One can see that these two sets of values can collide, and perhaps be untenable, for an international student who comes from a collectivistic society and seeks therapy in the United States.

An awareness of these cultural differences must inform mental health providers who work with international students. Considering cultural differences related to emotional expression is important, as is being mindful of embedded assumptions about the emphasis on emotional expression in therapy (Wei, Su, Carrera, Lin, & Yi, 2013).

Helpful strategies in providing mental health services to international students include:

1. Awareness of acculturation challenges the student faces, academic expectations the student may have, and the real limitations the international student may experience (including in many cases needing to be a full-time student in order to maintain visa status). Including being aware of the various ways American rugged individualism can manifest in college environments and might dampen sense of belongingness for international students.
2. Knowledge regarding collectivistic values and helping the student find ways of developing relationships and enhancing social support (both from others who share cultural values and from domestic students); includes encouraging educating domestic students on experiences of international students across campus.
3. Being more active, welcoming, and directive to international students, particularly at first.
4. Helping the student develop awareness and understanding of their identity development (culturally and racially) and situating that experience within the current student identity.
5. Being mindful that the student might experience instances of racism and discrimination, validating and processing these with the student, and if appropriate, inviting intentional dialogue about the challenges.
6. Being mindful of language proficiency, as well as differences in patterns of communication (including nonverbal communication and how it is interpreted through cultural lenses), which may be in the service of interpersonal harmony in the therapy relationship.
7. It is important for mental health providers to also be clearly aware of ways in which the institution and/or larger community may be less than welcoming.

Generally, it is helpful to look for culturally congruent coping methods. That said, it is also helpful to work with international students to help them identify different strategies they might need at various points in time, ultimately increasing the student's flexibility and coping skills repertoire while honoring their cultural values. Mori (2000) addresses more specific considerations for therapists working with international students.

Group approaches may also be helpful in addressing international students' needs, tapping into the importance of social support, decreasing isolation, and normalizing and validating their experiences. In these groups, it is important to address issues related to stigma, shame, and any misconceptions or concerns that exist about where information about them may be shared (e.g., with their government). International students may have concerns about confidentiality and privacy, and what these mean in the context of therapy. Practical considerations are also important, such as hosting the group away from the counseling center, in a setting more consistent with cultural norms and comfortable, as well as less stigmatizing, for international students. International students benefit from psychoeducational elements in group, such as learning cultural, interpersonal, and cultural skills (Yakunina et al., 2011), which they can then employ in their environment, and learning stress management.

Collaboration Across Campus

Counseling center professionals often receive referrals from colleagues on campus; close collaboration between offices is essential in working with international students. Faculty, residence hall staff, dean of students colleagues, and health center providers are people who may first spot an international student in distress. This student may first come to the attention of the campus Students of Concern Team. Just as awareness of cultural differences is essential to the counseling center professional, faculty and staff training related to cultural differences is an important element of campus education as we work with students from around the world. Multicultural training allows all to be aware of and understand important cultural elements to a situation involving an international student, taking into consideration cultural values, acculturation adjustment stress, and unique needs experienced by international students. Situations involving international students may then be addressed in a more nuanced and helpful manner for the student.

Strategies and Recommendations

- All readers are encouraged to review the suggestions outlined in the counseling center section of this chapter. Many of the suggestions, including awareness of institutional climate, acculturation challenges, and the impact of cultural values are relevant for anyone in the institution who assists international students.
- Offer workshops and orientation programs that provide information about the U.S. educational process and expectations of students (including definitions of acceptable collaboration among students and plagiarism), as well as cultural and social norms of the host culture.

- o Use peers, domestic students and/or more senior international students, who have successfully navigated campus (Abe, Talbot, & Geelhoed, 1998; Bradley, 2000).
- o Incorporate a compare-and-contrast approach to educational systems to heighten students' awareness of how they have learned to function in their home country's educational system and which of these skills may or may not transfer.
- Collaborate with student affairs and academic affairs departments:
  - o Offer programs at different times and locations, such as residence halls, academic departments, and the international students' office.
  - o Programs should connect the international student to others culturally similar to themselves, as well as to domestic students and international students from different cultures. This will help the student build social support while also develop a more accurate sense of the culture in the United States, develop stronger language skills, and enhance their skill and confidence in navigating their unfamiliar environment.
- Form contingency plans for significant behavioral and/or mental health issues.
  - o Develop policies and procedures and put in place in advance.
  - o Develop policies and processes regarding contact with family (such as what would trigger the institution to reach out to family; arrangements for translation services in case of language barriers; and plans regarding who would contact family and for what purpose).
  - o Develop these policies with input from campus partners such as the dean of students, university legal counsel, and mental health professionals.
  - o Consider including a provision in the student insurance policy that covers costs of sending the student home, if necessary.
  - o Consider an addition to institutional insurance that covers the cost of travel for a staff member who may need to accompany a student home. Though rare, there are some mental health-related emergency situations in which it is highly likely that the student may not be able to travel home safely or uneventfully.

References

Abe, J., Talbot, D. M., & Geelhoed, R. J. (1998). Effects of a peer program on international student adjustment. *Journal of College Student Development, 39*(6), 539–547.

Bradley, G. (2000). Responding effectively to the mental health needs of international students. *Higher Education, 39*, 417–433.

Guidry Lacina, J. (2002). Preparing international students for a successful social experience in higher education. In B. W. Speck & B. H. Carmical (Eds.), *New Directions for Higher Education: No. 117. Internationalizing higher education: Building vital programs on campuses* (pp. 21–28). San Francisco, CA: Jossey-Bass. doi:10.1002/he.43

Hamamura, T., & Laird, P. G. (2014). The effects of perfectionism and acculturation stress on levels of depression experienced by East Asian International students. *Journal of Multicultural Counseling and Development, 42*, 205–217.

Institute of International Education. (2014). *Open doors report on international educational exchange.* Retrieved from http://www.iie.org/opendoors

Iwamoto, D. K., & Liu, W. M. (2010). The impact of racial identity, ethnic identity, Asian values, and race related stress on Asian Americans and Asian International college students' psychological well-being. *Journal of Counseling Psychology, 57*(1), 79–91.

Jung, E., Hecht, M. L., & Wadsworth, B. C. (2007). The role of identity in international students' psychological well-being in the United States: A model of depression level, identity gaps, discrimination, and acculturation. *International Journal of Intercultural Relations, 31*, 605–624.

Lee, J.-Y., & Ciftci, A. (2013). Asian international students' sociocultural adaptation: Influence of multicultural personality, assertiveness, academic self-efficacy, and social support. *International Journal of Intercultural Relations*, 97–105. Retrieved from http://ex.doi.org/10.1016/j.ijintrel.2013.08.009

Liu, M. (2009). Addressing the mental health problems of Chinese international college students in the United States. *Advances in Social Work, 10*(1), 69–86.

Lui, P. P. (2014). Intergenerational cultural conflict, mental health, and educational outcomes among Asian and Latino/a Americans: Qualitative and meta-analytic review. *Psychological Bulletin, 141*(2), 1–43.

Masuda, A., Hayes, S. C., Twohig, M. P., Lillis, J., Fletcher, L. B., & Gloster, A. T. (2009). Comparing Japanese international students' and U.S. college students' mental health related stigmatizing attitudes. *Journal of Multicultural Counseling and Development, 37*, 178–189.

Misra, R., & Castillo, L. G. (2004). Academic stress among college students: Comparison of American and international students. *International Journal of Stress Management, 11*(2), 132–148.

Mori, S. C. (2000). Addressing the mental health concerns of international students. *Journal of Counseling and Development, 78*, 137–144. doi:10.1002/j.1556-6676.200.tb0271.x

Nordberg, S. S., Hayes, J. A., McAleavey, A. A., Castonguay, L. G., & Locke, B. D. (2013). Treatment utilization on college campuses: Who seeks help for what? *Journal of College Counseling, 16*, 258–274.

Olivas, M., & Li, C. (2006). Understanding stressors of international students in higher education: What college counselors and personnel need to know. *Journal of Instructional Psychology, 33*(3), 217–222.

Poyrazli, S., Kavanaugh, P. R., Baker, A., & Al-Timimi, N. (2004). Social support and demographic correlates of acculturative stress in international students. *Journal of College Counseling, 7*, 73–82.

Rosenthal, D. A., Russell, J., & Thomson, G. (2006). The health and well-being of International students at an Australian university. *Higher Education, 55*(1), 51–67.

Sümer, S., Poyrazli, S., & Grahame, K. (2008). Predictors of depression and anxiety among international students. *Journal of Counseling and Development, 86*, 429–437.

Tidwell, R., & Hanassab, S. (2007). New challenges for professional counsellors: The higher education international student population. *Counselling Psychology Quarterly, 20*(4), 313–324.

Wei, M., Su, J. C., Carrera, S., Lin, S-P., & Yi, F. (2013). Suppression and interpersonal harmony: A cross cultural comparison between Chinese and European Americans. *Journal of Counseling Psychology, 60*(4), 625–633.

Yakunina, E. S., Weigold, I. K., & McCarthy, A. S. (2011). Group counseling with international students: Practical, ethical, and cultural considerations. *Journal of College Student Psychotherapy, 25*, 67–81.

Yeh, C. J., & Inose, M. (2003). International students' reported English fluency, social support satisfaction, and social connectedness as predictors of acculturative stress. *Counseling Psychology Quarterly*, 16(1), 15–28.

Zhang, J., & Goodson, P. (2010). Acculturation and psychosocial adjustment of Chinese international students: Examining mediation and moderation effects. *International Journal of Intercultural Relations*, 35, 614–627.

SUSAN L. PRIETO-WELCH is the director of Counseling and Psychological Services at the Purdue University.

6

This chapter addresses issues pertaining to students who are at risk, possibly due to a psychological disability. Some of the challenges institutions of higher education confront in addressing at-risk students' struggles are identified, with specific focus placed on risk management and evolving legal mandates. No content is intended to represent legal advice.

Mental Health and Students at Risk

Alan B. Goodwin

College students "at risk" may be defined as individuals who lack a critical number of personal or social resources that are necessary to achieve college success. Newer psychotherapeutic and psychotropic treatments enable some students at risk to persevere who, in the past, would have withdrawn due to debilitating psychological conditions, such as psychosis, mania, autism spectrum disorders, depression, and anxiety. Some students are at risk primarily due to substance addiction, though many substance-addicted students are also at risk due to a co-occurring mental health problem (Brener, Hassan, & Barrios, 1999).

Students at risk can be among the most passionate, engaged, and well-liked students on campus. Nevertheless, students at risk often struggle socially, academically, and psychologically. Their inner turmoil is frequently exhibited in behaviors that intensify the struggle, leaving them feeling rejected, misunderstood, and isolated from the campus community.

This chapter explores the legal, social, and pedagogical interests institutions of higher education (IHEs) have in assisting students at risk to thrive.

Who Are the Students At Risk?

Students at risk include those who are socially isolated, irritable, and "threateningly erratic" in their behavior (Van Brunt, 2010). Some students at risk have a predictable and empirically demonstrated tendency to "spread" the risk-identified behaviors. A powerful and tragic example of this phenomenon, which might be termed "at-risk contagion," is observable in suicidal students. Students considering suicide tend to engage in self-destructive behaviors, often placing roommates and other students who are aware of their plight at risk of experiencing secondary trauma.

NEW DIRECTIONS FOR STUDENT SERVICES, no. 156, Winter 2016 © 2016 Wiley Periodicals, Inc.
Published online in Wiley Online Library (wileyonlinelibrary.com) • DOI: 10.1002/ss.20192

A comprehensive discussion of the ways at-risk contagion affects IHEs exceeds the scope of this chapter, but the example of suicidal ideation is worthy of attention here. Suicidal ideation leads to at-risk contagion in a self-perpetuating process. Lennings (1994) linked suicidal ideation to death by suicide by virtue of the former assisting in the development of cognitions that enable the latter.

Suicidal ideation has also been associated with life-threatening behaviors other than suicide attempts. Barrios, Everett, Simon, and Brener (2000) found that people who struggle with suicidal ideation also tend to be more likely to be involved in physical fights, engage in reckless driving, possess weapons, and behave in dangerous ways while intoxicated. Likewise, researchers have found that people who experience suicidal ideation are more likely to abuse substances (Brener, Hassan, & Barrios, 1999). Substance abuse is a vitally important indicator of potential danger to oneself because it can alter reality testing, impulse control, and recklessness. In terms of contagion, reckless and threatening behavior tends to activate anxiety responses in others (Holtz, Salama, Cardozo, & Gotway. 2002).

Behavior Intervention Teams and the Office for Civil Rights

One type of student at risk that has been identified is one who might pose a threat of physical harm to other students. Horrific incidents of mass violence at IHEs have led universities and community colleges to establish a group of professionals who regularly meet on campus to identify such students and seek to prevent violent acts (Bolante & Dykeman, 2015; Deisinger, Randazzo, & Nolan, 2014). These teams have had various labels such as Behavioral Intervention Team (BIT), Students of Concern Team, and Campus Assessment, Response, and Evaluation Team to name a few (Eells & Rockland-Miller, 2010).

The choice of how to name teams that identify potentially threatening students is not inconsequential. The team's name should clearly delimit the tasks in which the team engages. This clarity assists the team to define and restrict its activities, both of which facilitate improved performance over time. In addition, a descriptive team label helps the institutional community to understand and more effectively support the team, such as by assisting the team's information-gathering efforts. Nolan and Moncure (2012) allude to the value of transparency of such a team's practices by urging campuses to recognize the importance of adjusting campus policies and practices in ways that support the team's work and thus facilitate campus compliance with legal guidelines. Although violence prevention teams vary in the tasks in which they typically engage, for the sake of simplicity, this chapter refers to all such teams as BITs.

Students who exhibit at-risk behaviors often present BITs with complex social, legal, ethical, civic, and moral dilemmas. The U.S. Department of

Education's Office of Civil Rights (OCR) *Case Processing Manual* (2015) assists IHEs in complying with federal antidiscrimination laws.

OCR Jurisdiction and Enforcement of Federal Law. Through various legislative means, the OCR retains jurisdiction over both public and private colleges and universities. For example, Title II of the Americans with Disabilities Act (ADA) seeks to provide equal access to state and local government services (including education) to people with disabilities (Lannon, 2014). Section 504 of Section 5 of the Rehabilitation Act of 1973 extends the reach of the same antidiscrimination regulations to private entities that are recipients of federal financial assistance (Lannon & Sanghavi, 2011). One way this is achieved is by requiring equal access to education, sometimes by mandating the provision of reasonable accommodations to students with qualifying disabilities (OCR, 2010).

IHEs often claim to have difficulty conforming with federal guidelines because the OCR policy statements are not rigid or unequivocal descriptions of the law. Like any judicial or quasijudicial process, OCR decisions have often seemed difficult to predict, adding to the difficulty IHEs confront in crafting policies and taking action in particular cases (Grayson & Meilman, 2012). One example of how the OCR gradually shapes policy in unexpected ways involves ADA guidelines that IHEs had interpreted as requiring that accommodations be provided only to students who have self-identified as having a qualifying impairment. The OCR surprised some IHE administrators when it decided in favor of complainants who had not been registered as having a qualifying impairment (OCR, 2010).

Referred to as the Spring Arbor decision, this case did not alter the legal standard that requires a student to self-identify as having a disability in order to acquire accommodations. Spring Arbor did, however, clarify that even if a student had not self-identified as possessing a qualifying impairment, federal antidiscrimination guidelines prohibit an IHE from disadvantaging a student if the university knew the student had a qualifying impairment and if reasonable accommodations would have provided the student equal access to an education (OCR, 2010). Thus, enforcement of an IHE's policies and practices can be deemed discriminatory by the OCR even if the disadvantaged student had not formally sought accommodations through the IHE's disability services office.

Student Privacy Rights. Federal privacy statutes, state laws, and state professional licensing regulations all protect the privacy of students' personally identifiable information (PII; Styles, 2015). The information-gathering function of teams that address at-risk student concerns requires members to be knowledgeable of statutory and other privacy protections. The Family Educational Rights and Privacy Act (FERPA, 1974) is the primary federal law that protects the privacy of students' education records. Thus, education records are one form of PII. FERPA permits disclosure of students' PII to campus officials who possess a "legitimate educational interest" to view them (Styles, 2015). Under FERPA, "legitimacy" is broadly determined by the campus official who is tasked with being the custodian of the record. The primary focus in determining legitimacy is placed on whether PII access is needed to carry out the requesting official's institutional duties (U.S. Department of Health and Human Services, 2008).

FERPA distinguishes education records from "treatment records." Although both constitute types of PII, the latter are those made or maintained by campus medical or psychological professionals for the sole purpose of treating the student, with disclosure being permitted only under prescribed exceptional circumstances (see Title 34, Subtitle A, Chapter I, Part 99, Subpart D, section 99.31(a) of the Code of Federal Regulations; U.S. Department of Health and Human Services, 2008). Two of the commonly used exceptions permitting disclosure of PII under FERPA are a health and safety emergency and a "litigation exception" (such as a request attached to a judicial order or lawfully issued subpoena). If a treatment record is disclosed for any reason other than treatment, including provision directly to the student, the disclosed portion becomes permanently converted into an education record, thus receiving less protection from future disclosure than it would receive had it remained a treatment record (Styles, 2015).

In 2015, the Department of Education issued a clarification regarding FERPA's litigation exception (Styles, 2015). The clarification was prompted when a lawsuit filed by a University of Oregon student alleged the campus attorney wrongfully used the litigation exception to gain access to the student's treatment records (Pryal, 2015). To quell concerns that this use of FERPA may discourage students from seeking on-campus counseling, the Department of Education issued a statement urging that equivalent privacy protection be granted under FERPA for PII as exists for personal medical information under the Health Insurance Portability and Accountability Act (HIPAA; Styles, 2015). Styles (2015) articulated the view that IHE attorneys possess the requisite "legitimate educational interest" to access treatment records under the litigation exception only if commenced litigation "relates directly" to treatment or to payment for treatment.

The relevance HIPAA guidelines have to those IHE activities that are associated with students at risk varies with the nature of the IHE's delivery of health services. All IHEs benefit from consultation with their HIPAA compliance officer and legal counsel to identify potential compliance breaches that might arise out of the activities of any of the types of teams discussed in this chapter. Reinforcing this notion, Nolan and Moncure (2012) note that legal liabilities can arise if institutions merely form such teams but fail to continually revise practices and procedures in accord with evolving legal and social conditions.

Risk Assessment and Threat Assessment

BITs often confront a dilemma between the goal of strengthening public safety and the sometimes countervailing objective of protecting the individual rights of a person of concern (Mohandie & Hoffman, 2014). In addition to cases in which IHEs have been found to be discriminating against a person due to that person's disability, there may be other civil rights bases for such claims in the future. For example, a BIT could be accused of being more active in investigating underrepresented campus community members whose ethnicity, religion, or race allegedly caused the members of the BIT to view those individuals with more and unwarranted fear or suspicion. Finally, any BIT runs the risk of lawsuits alleging civil damages. Civil damages would involve such allegations as harm to reputation (slander or defamation), loss of job, and intentional or negligent infliction of emotional distress (e.g., see *Dennis L. Smith v. Iowa State University of Science and Technology and State of Iowa*, 2014).

Risk Assessment. Various on-campus violence prevention models exist. Threat assessment and risk assessment are two such approaches that are distinct in some ways, yet they share certain fundamental similarities (Meloy, Hart, & Hoffman, 2014). Meloy, Hoffmann, Guldimann, and James (2012) describe risk assessment as generally involving an assessment of the probability that a particular person will behave violently, based upon characteristics the person exhibits that are associated with violence. Keeney (2008) has described risk assessment as often referring to a more open, relational approach to assessing violence risk potential than does threat assessment. Risk assessment traditionally involved a single expert seeking to broadly assess a person's functional status (Keeney, 2008).

Risk assessment may be actuarial (structured), unstructured, or purely clinical (Conroy, 2012). Monahan (2008) has described the actuarial approach as one that relies on the search for the presence of empirically derived violence risk factors or traits, such as past violent behavior, psychopathy, relationship instability, impulsivity, lack of insight, and substance abuse history. Violence risk assessment requires that a balance be struck in assessing risk and protective factors in order to arrive at an estimate of the probability that a person will act out violently. As a result, in assessing likelihood of future violence, assessors would also look for the presence of known protective factors such as good performance in work or academic settings, close interpersonal relationships, emotion regulation, and community support (Conroy, 2012). Monahan (2008) described a three-stage actuarial risk assessment process: selecting risk factors, combining them in prescribed ways, and generating an estimate of risk.

Unstructured risk assessment relies not on identified factors but rather on the clinical judgment of the assessor. The reliability of unstructured risk assessment to predict future violence has been questioned (Monahan, 2008), but so have actuarial approaches (Campbell & DeClue, 2010; Murrie et al., 2009). In choosing between the two, Monahan (2008) cited the documented litigation benefits that have accrued to professionals who chose structured risk assessments as opposed to unstructured methods.

Threat Assessment and Management. Dunkle, Silverstein, and Warner (2008) identified the following common implementation stages for threat assessment teams (TATs) at IHEs: forming the team and defining members' roles/duties, assessing student behavior, choosing the best intervention strategy for a given situation, and collecting data to inform future team practices and policies. Deisinger and colleagues (2014) provided more specificity in terms of the threat assessment and management process at an IHE when they identified the following qualities that enhance effectiveness: enhancing centralized awareness of concerns, conducting a thorough and contextual assessment of identified concerns, developing an integrated case management plan, and, finally, monitoring and reassessing. In a broad sense, four categories of information have been identified as leading IHEs to consider initiating threat assessment and management: warning signs or "leakage," risk factors, stabilizing factors, and precipitating events (Mohandie, 2014).

Threat assessment processes have traditionally been more narrowly focused than those used in risk assessment and have been informed by the empirically derived methods used by the U.S. Secret Service and endorsed by the Federal Bureau of Investigations (Deisinger et al., 2014; Meloy et al., 2014). Reddy and her colleagues (2001) describe threat assessment as investigative and reflective of the belief that individuals who engage in targeted violence communicate their intention prior to the act, thus enabling prevention. The stated objective of prevention, as opposed to prediction, is often cited as a fundamental feature distinguishing threat assessment from violence risk assessment (Meloy et al., 2012).

Threat assessment generally involves information gathering about an individual by multiple participants working collaboratively (Keeney, 2008; Lake, 2007; Van Der Meer & Diekhuis, 2014). The threat assessment process occurs in four stages: identify a person of concern, investigate the person and situation, assess information gathered, and manage the person and situation to the degree needed to reduce the threat posed (Deisinger, 2008). Threat assessment has been described as case driven, fact based, and behaviorally focused (Meloy et al., 2014).

Deisinger and colleagues (2014) note that there has been variability in the degree to which TATs at IHEs operate with clear notions of purpose and process. The particular ways in which a given team conducts the investigation is of great importance. Some threat assessment practitioners describe the process as inherently skeptical and deductive (Keeney, 2008), requiring an awareness that interviewees may not be truthful (Van Der Meer & Diekhuis, 2014). Effective investigators must exhibit respect and professionalism (Mohandie, 2014).

TATs use a multidisciplinary team in an effort to improve the ability to assess for the presence of "warning behaviors," described as "toxic changes in patterns of behavior" that are associated with violence (Meloy et al., 2012). Meloy and his colleagues (2012) suggest that warning behaviors assist the team to determine whether an individual is on a "path toward violence" (Meloy et al., 2012, citing Calhoun & Weston, 2003). The "path" represents a lower threshold of proof of future violence risk and it is used in threat assessment but not in risk assessment (Keeney, 2008).

Withdrawal Policies and Civil Rights.   BITs seek to preserve the safety of the IHE community by identifying students at risk and determining how and whether to assist such students (Lannon, 2014). Withdrawal from the IHE is one tool BITs sometimes use to preserve community safety. In general, disability law requires institutional policies, such as medical withdrawal policies, to reflect equal rather than disparate treatment of students at risk who are known to have disabilities (Lannon, 2014). The OCR's 2010 letter of findings in the complaint brought against Spring Arbor University reflected this view (OCR, 2010).

Although every case is unique, the OCR seems to favor voluntary medical leave policies over involuntary medical leave policies (Lannon, 2014). The OCR Resolution Letter in a 2011 Georgetown University complaint offers a rich description of the federal legal compliance standards for voluntary medical withdrawal policies (OCR, 2011b). In addition to Lannon's (2014) clear and exhaustive legal analysis, an IHE is advised to review Lee's (2014) description of the interactive approach for assessing violence threat to others. Lee (2014) points out that an interactive method could assist a student to voluntarily withdraw, which would reduce the likelihood that a sustainable claim of discriminatory paternalism could later be brought.

Students at Risk of Harm to Others.   Styles (2015) recently reiterated the OCR policy that IHEs are granted broad latitude to prevent harm when there exists an informed, reasonable belief regarding an "articulable and significant threat" of harm to others. Lannon (2014) summarized the standards: an individualized assessment of the nature, severity, and history of this particular student's threatening behavior, obtained from medical professionals who possessed knowledge of the particular student and who used objective, science-informed processes. Lannon and Sanghavi (2011) explained that when a student with a disability is believed to present a threat of violence toward others, removal is permissible if there is a finding of a "high probability of substantial harm, not just a slightly increased, speculative, or remote risk" (p. 4).

Students at Risk of Harm to Self.   In 2011, a Department of Justice amendment to the ADA became effective, adding Section 35.139, which explicitly defines "direct threat" as involving threatened harm to others (U.S. Department of Justice, 2010). Since the establishment of a "direct threat" had, in the past, been a reliable defense to a disability discrimination allegation by students regardless of whether the threatened harm was to self or others, the apparent elimination of this defense in self-harm circumstances was believed by some to represent a significant change in the law (Lannon & Sanghavi, 2011).

It now seems more likely that the amendment was not intended to have the sweeping impact some feared. On the contrary, the prevailing view is that the OCR altered only the analysis that it recommends be used to examine the actions of an IHE that implements an involuntary medical withdrawal policy in a circumstance of only threat to self. Lannon (2014) explains that the change in the OCR's analysis is simply that the "direct threat" language is no longer used by the OCR in assessing an IHE's legal compliance in threat-to-self complaints. Lannon (2014) clarifies that the OCR's longstanding permissive view of an IHE taking steps to protect the safety, health, and well-being of the campus community—including the person of concern—remains intact. Although this level of specificity is provided in policy guidance, Lannon (2014) also advises IHEs to preserve flexibility in their policies so that they may be amended as the law evolves (see also Nolan & Moncure, 2012). The OCR's letter in a recent complaint brought against State University of New York Purchase exemplifies the description Lannon offered of the way in which the amended law is applied in complaints involving involuntary medical withdrawal policies in which there is only a threat of harm to self (OCR, 2011a).

Readmission After a Medical Withdrawal. In addition to the same nondiscriminatory standards required of withdrawal decisions, the OCR requires the IHE to provide "prompt and reasonable timeframes" within which the IHE shall determine the student's readiness for return (Lannon, 2014). In the Georgetown University Voluntary Resolution Letter, due process required that, at the time of the withdrawal, there be a clear description of the requirements for return to campus, including all required medical documentation (OCR, 2011b). Similarly, the 2013 OCR Letter to Princeton University reflected that the OCR grants broad discretion to IHEs to set conditions for return, if those conditions are reasonably related to a professional's science-informed, individualized assessment of the student's condition (OCR, 2013).

Strategies and Recommendations

In order for IHEs to adequately address the unique needs of students at risk:

- Campus administrators must understand legal mandates and must use that understanding to create an environment that is compassionate and that sincerely desires to be supportive of students' needs.
- Assist students exhibiting at-risk behaviors with policies and practices that embrace the value of diversity and that recognize the valuable contributions any student can make to the campus community if properly supported.
- Encourage faculty to integrate teaching methods that respect and reward diverse learning styles, thus more effectively assisting students at risk to reach their academic potential.

- Serve both the campus community and students exhibiting at-risk behaviors by adopting withdrawal policies that reward, rather than punish, students who voluntarily suspend academic pursuits in favor of establishing a higher level of personal functioning.

References

Barrios, L. C., Everett, S. A., Simon, T. R., & Brener, N. D. (2000). Suicide ideation among US college students associations with other injury risk behaviors. *Journal of American College Health*, *48*(5), 229–233. doi:10.1080/07448480009599309

Bolante, R., & Dykeman, C. (2015). Threat assessment in community colleges. *Journal of Threat Assessment and Management*, *2*(1), 23. doi:10.1037/tam0000033

Brener, N. D., Hassan, S. S., & Barrios, L. C. (1999). Suicidal ideation among college students in the United States. *Journal of Consulting and Clinical Psychology*, *67*(6), 1004–1008. doi:10.1037/0022-006X.67.6.1004

Calhoun, T., & Weston, S. (2003). *Contemporary threat management*. San Diego, CA: Specialized Training Services.

Campbell, T. W., & DeClue, G. (2010). Flying blind with naked factors: Problems and pitfalls in adjusted-actuarial sex-offender risk assessment. *Open Access Journal of Forensic Psychology*, *2*, 75–101. Retrieved from http://www.forensicpsychologyunb ound.ws/OAJFP/Volume_2__2010_files/Campbell%20%26%20DeClue%202010.pdf

Conroy, M. A. (2012). *Assessing and managing violence risk*. Presentation at the American Academy of Forensic Psychology training, Irvine, CA.

Deisinger, E. R. D., Randazzo, M. R., & Nolan, J. J. (2014). Threat assessment and management in higher education: Enhancing the standard of care in the academy. In J. R. Meloy & J. Hoffman (Eds.), *International handbook of threat assessment* (pp. 107–125). New York, NY: Oxford.

Deisinger, G. (2008, October 17). *Critical incident response team threat management process*. Presentation at the Association for University and College Counseling Center Directors Annual Conference, Fort Worth, TX.

Dennis, L. Smith, v. Iowa State University of Science and Technology and State of Iowa, Appellants, No. 12–1182. Decided July 18, 2014. Retrieved from http://caselaw. findlaw.com/ia-supreme%20court/1673157.html

Dunkle, J. H., Silverstein, Z. B., & Warner S. L. (2008). Managing violent and other troubling students: The role of threat assessment teams on campus. *Journal of College and University Law*, *34*(3), 585–636.

Eells, G. T., & Rockland-Miller, H. S. (2010). Assessing and responding to disturbed and disturbing students: Understanding the role of administrative teams in institutions of higher education. *Journal of College Student Psychotherapy*, *25*(1), 8–23. doi:10.1080/87568225.2011.532470

Family Educational Rights and Privacy Act of 1974, 34 CFR 99.31(a).

Grayson, P., & Meilman, P. (2012). Mandatory leaves in limbo. *Journal of College Student Psychotherapy*, *26*(4), 253–255. Doi:10.1080/87568225.2012.711132

Holtz, T. H., Salama, B., Cardozo, B. L., & Gotway, C. A. (2002). Mental health status of human rights workers, Kosovo, June 2000. *Journal of Traumatic Stress*, *15*(5), 389–395. doi:10.1023/A:1020133308188

Keeney, M. (2008, October 17). *Comparison of clinical risk assessment and threat assessment*. Presentation at Association for University and College Counseling Center Directors annual conference, Fort Worth, TX.

Lake, P. F. (2007, June). The Chronicle Review: Higher education called to account. *Chronicle of Higher Education*, *53*(43). Retrieved from http://chronicle.com/article/Higher-Education-Called-to/26751/

Lannon, P. G. (2014). Direct threat and caring for students at risk for self-harm: Where we stand now. *NACUANOTES*, *12*(8). Retrieved from http://www.higheredcompliance.org/resources/SelfHarm.pdf

Lannon, P. G., & Sanghavi, E. (2011). New Title II regulations regarding direct threat: Do they change how colleges and universities should treat students who are threats to themselves? *NACUANOTES*, *10*(1). Retrieved from http://counsel.cua.edu/nacuanotes/titleIIregulations.cfm

Lee, B. A. (2014). Dealing with students with psychiatric disorders on campus: Legal compliance and prevention strategies. *Journal of College & University Law*, *40*(3) 425–441.

Lennings, C. J. (1994). A cognitive understanding of adolescent suicide. *Genetic, Social, and General Psychology Monographs*, *120*(3), 289–307.

Meloy, J. R., Hart, S. D., & Hoffmann, J. (2014). Threat assessment and threat management. In J. R. Meloy & J. Hoffman (Eds.), *International handbook of threat assessment* (pp. 3–17). New York: Oxford.

Meloy, J. R., Hoffmann, J., Guldimann, A., & James, D. (2012). The role of warning behaviors in threat assessment: An exploration and suggested typology. *Behavioral Sciences & the Law*, *30*(3), 256–279. doi:10.1002/bsl.999

Monahan, J. (2008). Structured risk assessment of violence. In R. I. Simon & K. Tardiff (Eds.), *Textbook of violence assessment and management* (pp. 17–34). Washington, DC: American Psychiatric Publishing.

Mohandie, K. (2014). Threat assessment in schools. In J. R. Meloy & J. Hoffman (Eds.), *International handbook of threat assessment* (pp. 126–141). New York: Oxford.

Mohandie, K., & Hoffman, J. (2014). Legal issues in threat management. In J. R. Meloy & J. Hoffman (Eds.), *International handbook of threat assessment* (pp. 67–79). New York: Oxford.

Murrie, D. C., Boccaccini, M. T., Turner, D. B., Meeks, M., Woods, C., & Tussey, C. (2009). Rater (dis)agreement on risk assessment measures in sexually violent predator proceedings: Evidence of adversarial allegiance in forensic evaluation?. *Psychology, Public Policy, and Law*, *15*(1), 19–53. doi:10.1037/a0014897

Nolan, J. J., & Moncure, T. M., Jr. (2012). The legal side of campus threat assessment and management: What student counselors need to know. *Journal of College Student Psychotherapy*, *26*(4), 322–340. doi:10.1080/87568225.2012.711182

Office of Civil Rights. (2010, December 16). Complaint No. 15-10-2098. [Letter to Spring Arbor University]. Cleveland, OH: U.S. Department of Education, Office for Civil Rights. Retrieved from http://www.bazelon.org/LinkClick.aspx?fileticket=WGmoOxFqnto%3D&tabid=313

Office of Civil Rights. (2011a, January 14). State University of New York, Case No. 02-10-2181. [Letter to Purchase College]. New York, NY: U. S. Department of Education, Office for Civil Rights. Retrieved from https://www.ncherm.org/documents/OCRLetter_PurchaseCollege.pdf

Office of Civil Rights. (2011b, October 13). Voluntary resolution agreement, Complaint No. 11-11-2044. [Letter to Georgetown University]. Washington, DC: U. S. Department of Education, Office for Civil Rights. Retrieved from http://www.bazelon.org/LinkClick.aspx?fileticket=ttN4vzvSIkc%3D&tabid=313

Office of Civil Rights. (2013, January 18). Complaint No. 02-12-2155. [Letter to Princeton University]. New York, NY: U. S. Department of Education, Office for Civil Rights. Retrieved from U. S. Department of Education, Office of Civil Rights. (2013). Letter to Princeton University, Complaint No. 02-12-2155, 2, Jan. 18, 2013.

Pryal, K. R. G. (2015, March). Raped on campus? Don't trust your college to do the right thing. *Chronicle of Higher Education*. Retrieved from http://chronicle.com/article/Raped-on-Campus-Don-t-Trust/228093/

Reddy, M., Borum, R., Berglund, J., Vossekuil, B., Fein, R., & Modzeleski, W. (2001). Evaluating risk for targeted violence in schools: Comparing risk assessment, threat assessment, and other approaches. *Psychology in the Schools, 38*(2) 157–172. doi:10.1002/pits.1007

Styles, K. M. (2015, August). Dear colleague letter to school officials at institutions of higher education [Dear colleague letter: Protecting student medical records]. Washington, DC: U.S. Department of Education. Retrieved from http://ptac.ed.gov/sites/default/files/DCL%20Final%20Signed-508.pdf

U.S. Department of Education, Office for Civil Rights. (2015). *Case processing manual.* Washington, DC: Government Printing Office. Retrieved from http://www2.ed.gov/about/offices/list/ocr/docs/ocrcpm.pdf

U. S. Department of Health and Human Services. (2008). *Joint guidance on the application of the Family Educational Rights and Privacy Act (FERPA) and the Health Insurance Portability and Accountability Act of 1996 (HIPAA) to student health records.* Washington, DC: U. S. Department of Education, Family Policy Compliance Office. Retrieved from http://www2.ed.gov/policy/gen/guid/fpco/doc/ferpa-hipaa-guidance.pdf

U. S. Department of Justice, Civil Rights Division. (2010). Final rule: Nondiscrimination on the basis of disability in state and local government services. *Federal Register, 75*(178) 56164–56236. Retrieved from http://www.gpo.gov/fdsys/pkg/FR-2010-09-15/html/2010-21821.htm

Van Brunt, B. (2010). Helping at-risk students build resilience. *Student Affairs Leader, 38*(3) 1–6. Retrieved from http://brianvanbrunt.com/wp-content/uploads/2013/03/helping-at-risk-students.pdf

Van Der Meer, B. B., & Diekhuis, M. L. (2014). Collecting and assessing information for threat assessment. In J. R. Meloy & J. Hoffman (Eds.), *International handbook of threat assessment* (pp. 54–66). New York: Oxford.

ALAN B. GOODWIN is a California licensed psychologist and attorney and mediator certified by the Los Angeles County Bar Association. He served as the director of the Student Counseling Services center at California Lutheran University for 10 years, beginning in 2006. He maintains a psychotherapy and consultation practice in Encino, California.

7

Tragedy can strike a college campus in unpredictable and often horrific ways that may lead to traumatic responses for individuals and the entire campus community. Crises on campus demand an appropriate response to support the community, provide assistance to affected individuals and guide healing efforts.

Mental Health Aspects of Responding to Campus Crises

Christopher Flynn, Micky M. Sharma

A crisis on campus can be precipitated by a range of events that are unexpected, have significant consequences to individuals and the community, and may easily overwhelm the existing structures in place to support students, faculty, staff, and the greater university community. By definition "a time of intense difficulty, trouble or danger" (Oxford Dictionaries, 2015), a crisis brings with it a confrontation with danger that may have physical, psychological, and economic consequences for the individual and the community. The precipitating event may occur in the greater community or on campus, but the rippling effects may be felt across the boundaries of both and extend to family members and alumni across the country and the world. Sadly, most of us will be affected by a traumatic event and its consequences at some time; a large review of the disaster literature (Norris, Friedman, & Watson, 2002) estimated that 69% of us will be exposed to a traumatic event in our lives, and a significant percentage will experience related disruption in our emotional equilibrium (15–24% of those exposed to trauma).

The examples of crises on campus are many and varied; all campus professionals can bring to mind some defining crises that have occurred in academic communities in the past 2 decades. Each of these painful events merits careful study, although the intent here is a more general review of the types of disasters that might befall campuses, the potential mental health consequences, and requisite interventions that follow.

A campus may be affected by natural disasters, vehicular accidents, and death(s) of students, faculty, and staff. Natural disasters, including tornadoes, hurricanes, and flooding, may have effects that involve an entire community in which the university is located. In August 2005, Hurricane Katrina devastated the Gulf Coast from Florida to Louisiana, caused the deaths of over 1,500 individuals, and displaced another 1 million people;

NEW DIRECTIONS FOR STUDENT SERVICES, no. 156, Winter 2016 © 2016 Wiley Periodicals, Inc.
Published online in Wiley Online Library (wileyonlinelibrary.com) • DOI: 10.1002/ss.20193

all of the universities in New Orleans were closed for the fall semester. In April 2011, tornadoes struck Tuscaloosa, Alabama, leaving 41 dead, including 6 students at the University of Alabama.

Transportation-related accidents may result in fatality and injury to students, faculty, and staff. The tragic crash of Southern Airways Flight 932 on November 11, 1970 killed 45 members of the Marshall University football team (students and coaches), 25 community boosters, and 5 crew members. Seventy children lost at least one parent and 18 children were orphaned by the crash. Motor vehicle accidents are the most common cause of death of college students (Turner, Bauerle, & Keller, 2011) and often an accident may involve more than one student; on April 22, 2015, seven nursing students from Georgia Southern University were traveling when their cars were struck by a tractor trailer, killing five and injuring two.

Accidents on campus with injury or death may involve one campus member or many. The death of Elizabeth Shin, now attributed to an accidental death by fire, had widespread effects on the campus of the Massachusetts Institute of Technology in 2000. At Texas A & M, the annual bonfire was a campus tradition; the collapse of the structure on November 18, 1999, resulted in the death of 12 current and former students and injured 27.

Both of the authors have directed counseling centers at universities that were affected by a particular type of tragedy when a suicidal student focused his rage on the university community and murdered classmates and faculty. On April 16, 2007, Seung-Hui Cho shot 49 members of the Virginia Tech community, killing 32, before shooting himself as the police approached. Less than a year later, Steven Kazmierczak entered a classroom at Northern Illinois University (NIU) on February 14, 2008, shot and killed 5 students and injured 21 others before killing himself as the police responded. Tragically, there have been similar events on or near college campuses and in K–12 schools since then, including the killings of 27 children and teachers at Sandy Hook Elementary school on December 14, 2012.

Response to Tragedy

Each of the tragedies recounted here brought widespread distress to the university community, to those connected to the campus community from a distance, and to the wider world who were witness to tragedy though media exposure. Initial reactions to a traumatic event include disbelief and shock; it is very difficult to integrate these disastrous events into our daily experience of being in the world. Grief, sadness, anxiety, and fear often follow these events and the intensity of these emotions will vary as a function of a number of factors including proximity to the event, closeness to the victims who were directly affected, as well as individual variability in how we understand the tragedy.

In order to conceptualize the ramifications of tragedy for the campus, the Population Exposure Model (U.S. Department of Health and Human

Services, 2004) provides a helpful framework. The model posits that the traumatic event affects groups differently, from those most directly affected (group A) to those who feel the effects in the wider community (group E). Group A is composed of those who are killed and injured and the families and loved ones of these campus members. Extending outward in concentric circles, the impacts will be felt by (B) those who were direct witnesses to the event who escaped physical injury, (C) more extended family and friends, as well as first responders who intervened at the scene or those who worked directly with bereaved family members and friends, (D) those tasked with responding to the scene, such as mental health providers, clergy or emergency health care providers, and (E) the community at large and others with connection to the victims or campus.

In a university community, the number of those affected can grow exponentially. As an example of this, Virginia Tech is a university community of 30,000 students and 7,500 faculty and staff. In a survey conducted following the shootings of 2007, almost 80% of the students surveyed knew a student or faculty member who was injured or killed; this ranged from 9.1% who were close to one of the deceased, 29.1% who were friends or acquaintances, and far more who were distantly connected (Hughes et al., 2011). Despite being a fairly large university, the majority of the campus was only one degree of separation from a victim of the tragedy. Thus, the entire community of campus and town reverberated from the effects of the shooting—as did alumni and others with a connection to the university.

With the Population Exposure Model as a heuristic, the response to any campus tragedy must encompass the entire community as individuals who may suffer emotionally in the aftermath. A further challenge for the university is that its administrators, mental health providers, faculty, and staff will be personally affected by the trauma and will also be thrust into the role of helping others heal. For mental health professionals on campus, their roles will vary depending on the circumstances of the event and the resources available to the university, but they are typically central to the response effort. In the initial response, there will be multiple interventions directed at different populations and a strong emphasis on coordinated collaborative efforts with the entire response team (Watson et al., 2011).

Immediate Response and Intervention. The immediate response must be directed to care for the injured and for the families and loved ones of the deceased. Police and emergency personnel will usually be first on the scene and will direct emergency efforts. As the injured are stabilized medically, the awareness of their psychological needs must also be assessed. The majority of survivors with posttraumatic stress report that their symptoms began the same day as the traumatic event and 94% reported that symptoms began in the same week as the event (North, 2003). Bereaved family members will require immediate attention and support; a key phrase is "protect, direct, and connect" (Myers & Wee, 2005): they must be directed to a protected environment where they will be insulated from the media and well-meaning others, given provisions for basic physiological needs, and connected with other family members and loved ones.

Mental health professionals can begin Psychological First Aid (Brymer et al., 2006) immediately with affected community members. Psychological First Aid is widely recommended as an evidence-based practice for application following trauma (Watson, 2008). Psychological First Aid provides emotionally distraught survivors with a human connection to assist in calming and orienting them to care for their immediate needs. The provider offers practical guidance for meeting their basic needs; linking the survivor to extant social support networks, including family and friends; assessing and providing information for other resources in the community, including mental health services; and encouraging active problem solving. The on-campus counseling center may become a central support for the student and university community and survivors may be directed to the center for immediate Psychological First Aid.

The clinicians from the campus counseling center may also provide on-site Psychological First Aid at areas where survivors and other students have gathered. In addition to providing assistance to community members who are present, the clinicians will be able to gain information about other individuals in need of assistance who are not physically present, which can help guide outreach efforts to groups and individuals in greatest need. It is equally likely that the needs of the survivors may require more support than on-campus professionals can provide, so coordination with local and regional resources, including local mental health centers, the American Red Cross, and other networks, will be required. It is very difficult to make this coordination happen in the middle of a crisis, so previously negotiated memoranda of understanding with local and state mental health agencies and universities are very helpful. On one occasion where the authors responded to a tragic event, the governor of the state had to issue an emergency directive waiving the state licensure requirement in order to allow out-of-state providers to respond.

Communications.   In the aftermath of tragedy, there is an amplification of the intrinsic human need for knowledge and communication about the event, so crisis communication has great importance (Hincker, 2014). At a minimum, basic information about the tragedy can allay anxiety and communicate messages of relative risk and safety. Crisis communication can direct survivors and community members to immediate resources that provide basic necessities. With electronic resources and social media, campus members can be directed to relevant online resources and alerted to important events on campus. Hincker (2014) notes that key facts should be repeated again and again to ensure that all are informed and that the myriad topics of importance are addressed in an open and transparent manner.

Institutional communications regarding mental health issues should be timely and focused; many of the professional organizations of mental health providers quickly issue fact sheets and bulletins regarding psychological responses to tragedy that can be made available in print and on a website. In the midst of crisis, there may be ill-informed rumors and misunderstandings that can divide the community; clear and consistent communication can bring the community together and aid healing and resilience. Accurate and regular communication from the institution will address the multitude of media inquiries that will arise. The dissemination of timely and relevant information undergirds all outreach efforts.

Ongoing Needs Assessment.   Needs assessment for the campus is both an immediate and an ongoing process. This becomes a foundation for intervention planning after the initial response to critical needs. For the mental health provider, a needs assessment will begin the process of anticipating the campus requirements for initial triage and continuing treatment, as well as the assessment of the adequacy of resources. In the aftermath of tragedy, there is typically a surge in requests for counseling as individuals and families cope with loss, grief, and recovery. Following the tragedies at both Virginia Tech and NIU, there was a dramatic increase in counseling center usage immediately thereafter that continued in the following years—this continuation may follow the increased visibility of counseling on campus as well as reflect increases reported by counseling centers nationally.

Mental Health in the Aftermath of Tragedy

Tragedy brings with it a tremendous variety of responses, reactions, and concerns. It is expected that those most directly affected by tragedy will have very strong reactions and that the course of these reactions will vary in severity and duration. The emotional distress that individuals experience will likely include grief and sadness for the injured, deceased, and their loved ones. These repercussions of tragedy can reverberate in one's psyche for a long period of time, and survivors and loved ones may experience overwhelming stress when trying to integrate the unthinkable into their life and experience as time passes. By and large, these reactions are transient and slowly resolve over time as affected individuals gradually reenter and resume vocational and social involvements. However, this may not be the case for some of those most affected by tragedy, and their distress and responses may be severe and interfere with their previous level of functioning. These individuals may need treatments that serve to aid them to cope and function in their lives. Mental health professionals understand and categorize the individual response to tragedy by the intensity, severity, and length of reaction; assessments may help determine potential treatments and to guide research.

Resources and messaging directed to survivors of traumatic events in the immediate and near aftermath can assist with their emotional response. Survivors should be instructed to honor their emotional response. The healing process can move more smoothly when survivors work to accept how they are feeling and process those emotions. Survivors need to know that the healing process is not linear—it will often ebb and flow as survivors experience different emotions over time. Each survivor's response will be unique and specific to their experience of the trauma (U.S. Department of Health & Human Services, 2004).

The immediate stress reaction to trauma can include emotional, behavioral, cognitive, and physical effects. Emotionally, individuals experience shock and disbelief following the tragedy in addition to anxiety or fearfulness. As the awareness of the losses becomes evident, sadness and grief that are almost palpable in intensity are present. Physically, individuals may feel faint or dizzy, may experience nausea and gastrointestinal distress, and may become hyperaroused and agitated. In the aftermath, sleep disturbances, including insomnia or hypersomnia, are often present. Behaviorally, survivors of trauma may withdraw socially, isolating themselves and avoiding reminders of trauma. Individuals may increase their use of substances, including alcohol, tobacco, or other drugs. Cognitively, experiences of trauma make concentration difficult and individuals report difficulties with memory. They may feel confused and disoriented, and have difficulty in planning or problem solving. They may experience recurrent and intrusive memories of the event or suffer flashbacks in which the event is reexperienced.

Individual survivors of traumatic events may experience some or all of these effects. The effects may vary in intensity and duration and may feel so overwhelming that psychosocial functioning becomes difficult or impossible. When there is significant impairment in functioning coupled with extreme distress, individuals may meet the criteria for a psychiatric diagnosis (American Psychiatric Association [APA], 2013). Individuals who experience significant, disruptive symptoms (such as intrusive thoughts or flashbacks to the event, sleep disturbances, or difficulty concentrating) for the first several weeks following the incident may meet the criteria to be diagnosed with acute stress disorder (ASD). When those symptoms persist and continue to be disruptive to normal functioning for longer than a month, the more commonly known diagnosis of posttraumatic stress disorder (PSTD) might be applicable.

Not everyone with ASD will go on to develop PTSD; Bryant and colleagues (Bryant, Friedman, Spiegel, Ursano, & Strain, 2010) reported that half of the individuals with ASD do not go on to develop PTSD. However, acute stress disorder may predict the development of PTSD after the initial month; examining PTSD in survivors of the Oklahoma City bombing, North (2003) noted that the vast majority reported that symptoms began immediately after the bombing, 76% on the first day, 94% within the first week, and 98% in the first month. In their review of the relevant literature, Bryant and colleagues (2010) noted that prevalence rates for the full diagnosis of ASD were 7–28% with a mean of 13%; including individuals with partial symptoms raised the prevalence to 10–32% with a mean of 23%.

North (2003) estimates the upper range for a diagnosis of PTSD to be 34% of survivors of the Oklahoma City bombing. By diagnostic criteria, ASD ends at 1 month, but the length of PTSD can be much longer and can become a chronic disorder with half of those individuals diagnosed with PTSD experiencing symptoms lasting a year or longer and as many as one third lasting a decade or more (North, 2003).

Following tragedy, women are more likely to be diagnosed with a stress disorder and/or depression than are men, but men are more likely to be diagnosed with a substance abuse disorder; this parallels the similar difference in elevated rates of depression for women and substance abuse for men in the general population. Individuals with a prior history of depression or substance abuse are more likely to see these disorders exacerbated or continuing after a tragedy (North, 2003).

Individuals do not have to be present at the immediate scene of the tragedy to experience symptoms of a stress disorder. In a study of Virginia Tech students present on campus during the shooting, Hughes et al. (2011) note that the predictors of posttraumatic stress symptoms were closeness to someone who was injured or killed as well as not being able to contact friends in the immediate aftermath of the shooting. Similarly, family members of those directly affected can develop symptoms of a stress disorder as may those who were first responders or treating health professionals providing treatment to those directly affected by trauma.

After the Tragedy: Responding to the Campus

After a large-scale traumatic event has affected a campus community, it is important to prepare all members of the community for the resumption of classes and campus activities. This is of increased importance when a campus has canceled classes or closed following a traumatic event. The university should be intentional in developing a plan to prepare faculty, staff, and students for its return to regular operations; a detailed description of these plans is outlined in *Enough is Enough: A Student Affairs Perspective on Preparedness and Response to a Campus Shooting* (Hemphill & Hephner LaBanc, 2010).

Faculty and staff will need preparation to resume their work with students and to return to work after a campus tragedy. As members of the campus community, faculty and staff will each have been affected by the tragedy to varying degrees; therefore, they can benefit from an awareness of resources to assist them in their own healing. Resources may include an on-campus employee assistance program as well as information regarding off-campus mental health providers. Preparatory meetings can be helpful to all faculty and staff and may be grouped by their academic/staff areas. These meetings can be conducted by on-campus counselors or other mental health professionals and will allow the counselors to provide Psychological First Aid to the faculty and staff.

Throughout their careers, many faculty members have become accustomed to being the "expert" at the front of a classroom; however, the resumption of classes following a campus tragedy will leave some faculty struggling with how to address students about what has transpired. These meetings with faculty and staff are an opportunity to provide guidance for their interaction with students, present resources with which to refer students for assistance, and provide support for the individual faculty and staff. The elements of Psychological First Aid indicate that faculty and staff should be provided with practical information and logistics about the resumption of all campus operations as well as information about emotional healing and possible responses to trauma. The faculty and staff should be educated about signs of emotional distress they may see in students, in themselves, and in one another.

As students return to campus and the classroom following a large-scale traumatic event, having a clinician in the initial meeting of each class can be an excellent intervention to assist students in their transition (Sharma, Bershad, & LaBanc, 2010). The clinician serves as an on-site support person for the faculty member who is teaching the class and will be readily available should anyone become significantly distressed during the class meeting. The clinician's role is to provide Psychological First Aid and not to provide mental health counseling to the entire class. The clinician can provide psychoeducation about the process of healing and effects of trauma, inform students about on-campus resources, and be available for any student who wishes to talk to a counselor immediately. This intervention expresses a strong message of care and concern to all students. In the aftermath of a tragedy, students will have their sense of psychological security harmed, and the presence of clinicians in the classroom can help to enhance their trust in the healing process.

The use of social media is widespread across all college campuses. Social media provide instant access to information to all members of the campus community. In the aftermath of tragedy, this can be advantageous to inform students about meetings or classes that have been altered or that may be helpful to attend. Many students use social media as a way to connect and support one another. Being able to connect and receive support from fellow students is of critical importance following tragedy. It can also be a venue for the university to share accurate information and dispel myths and rumors. However, social media can also be problematic for the institution; inaccurate information may be shared very quickly via social media platforms, which can increase the anxiety experienced by faculty, staff, and students. Further, there will be members of the community who wish to "take a break" from the constant updates that social media can provide following a tragedy. These individuals may experience the social media updates as frustrating or as exacerbating their distress and should be supported in making that choice.

Strategies and Recommendations

- Identify staff across departments who have the requisite skill set to assist during a large-scale crisis. Staff who have demonstrated an ability to perform effectively when under highly stressful conditions should be identified.
- Have counseling center staff and any adjunct mental health units trained in Psychological First Aid.
- Have staff from multiple campus units participate in tabletop scenarios to gain experience and identify potential deficits in response plans and protocols.
- Establish clear communication guidelines for both internal and external communications to be followed after a large scale event.
- Institutional leaders should be familiar with the Federal Emergency Management Agency (FEMA) training and organizational tools; colleges and universities engaged in proactive emergency management will be better prepared to respond to any traumatic event (see http://www.fema.gov/national-preparedness-system).

References

American Psychiatric Association. (2013). *Diagnostic and statistical manual of mental disorders* (5th ed.). Arlington, VA: Author.

Bryant, R. A., Friedman, M. J., Spiegel, D., Ursano, R., & Strain, J. (2010). A review of acute stress disorder in DSM-5. *Depression and Anxiety, 28*(9), 1–16.

Brymer, M., Jacobs, A., Layne, C., Pynoos, R., Ruzek, J., Steinberg, A., ... Watson, P. (2006). *Psychological first aid: =Field operations guide* (2nd ed.). Washington, DC: National Child Traumatic Stress Network and National Center for PTSD. Retrieved from http://www.nctsn.org/sites/default/files/pfa/english/1-psyfirstaid_final_complete_ma nual.pdf

Hemphill, B. O., & Hephner LaBanc, B. (Eds.). (2010). *Enough is enough: A student affairs perspective on preparedness and response to a campus shooting*. Sterling, VA: Stylus Publishing.

Hincker, L. (2014). Crisis communications: Lessons learned from the Virginia Tech tragedy. In G. M. Bataille & D. I. Cordova (Eds.). *Managing the unthinkable: Crisis preparation and response for campus leaders*. Sterling, VA: Stylus Publishing.

Hughes, M., Brymer, M., Chiu, W. T., Fairbank, J. A., Jones, R. T., Pynoos, R. S., ... Kessler, R. C. (2011). Posttraumatic stress among students after the shootings at Virginia Tech. *Psychological Trauma: Theory, Research, Practice and Policy, 3*, 403–411.

Myers, D. G., & Wee, D. F. (2005). *Disaster mental health services: A primer for practitioners*. New York: Brunner-Routledge.

Norris, F. H., Friedman, M. J., & Watson, P. J. (2002). 60,000 disaster victims speak, Part 1. An empirical review of the empirical literature: 1981–2001. *Psychiatry, 65*, 207–239.

North, C. (2003). Psychiatric epidemiology of disaster responses. In R. J. Ursano & A. E. Norwood (Eds.), *Trauma and disaster responses and management*. Washington, DC: American Psychiatric Association.

Oxford Dictionaries (2015). Retrieved from http://www.oxforddictionaries.com/us

Sharma, M., Bershad, C., & LaBanc, D. (2010). Counseling during a campus-wide crisis. In B. Hemphill & B. Hephner LaBanc (Eds.), *Enough is enough: A student affairs perspective on preparedness and response to a campus shooting.* Sterling, VA: Stylus Publishing.

Turner, J., Bauerle, J., & Keller, A. (2011). Alcohol-related vehicular death rates for college students in the Commonwealth of Virginia. *Journal of American College Health, 59*, 323–326.

U.S. Department of Health and Human Services. (2004). *Mental health response to mass violence and terrorism: A training manual* (DHHS Publication No. SMA 3959). Rockville, MD: Center for Mental Health Services, Substance Abuse and Mental Health Administration.

Watson, P. J. (2008). Psychological first aid. In M. Blumenfield & R. J. Ursano (Eds.), *Intervention and Rresilience after Mmass Ttrauma.* Cambridge: Cambridge University Press.

Watson, P. J., Brymer, M. J., & Bonanno, G. A. (2011). Postdisaster psychological intervention since 9/11. *American Psychologist, 66*, 482–494.

CHRISTOPHER FLYNN *is director of the Thomas E. Cook Counseling Center at Virginia Tech.*

MICKY M. SHARMA *is director of Counseling and Consultation Services at The Ohio State University.*

NEW DIRECTIONS FOR STUDENT SERVICES • DOI: 10.1002/ss

8

This chapter describes why resilience and mental health deserve more attention in efforts to increase student retention. The chapter offers practical suggestions for campus administrators and others.

Promoting Resilience, Retention, and Mental Health

Daniel Eisenberg, Sarah Ketchen Lipson, Julie Posselt

Access to college has increased in recent decades, but completion rates have not (Bound, Lovenheim, & Turner, 2010; Bowen, Chingos, & Mcpherson, 2009). The national 6-year bachelor's graduation rate remained less than 60% in 2013 (Kena et al., 2014), and these rates are significantly lower among Black, Latinx, and low-income students (Bound et al., 2010; Snyder & Dillow, 2013). Although policymakers and researchers have made considerable efforts to address barriers to degree completion, one important factor has not been fully considered in the national dialogue: student mental health.

The prevalence of mental health problems among college students has increased steadily (Twenge et al., 2010; see also Chapter 2 in this volume). Roughly one third of undergraduates have clinically significant symptoms of mental health problems such as depression and anxiety (Eisenberg, Hunt, & Speer, 2013). Increased access to effective mental health care during childhood and adolescence has created new opportunities for young people with preexisting mental health conditions to enroll in college. Lack of resilience is also cited as contributing to what some refer to as the "campus mental health crisis" (Eiser, 2011; Gabriel, 2010; Schwartz & Kay, 2009). Resilience refers to the ability of people to achieve "good outcomes in spite of serious threats to adaptation or development" (Masten, 2001, p. 228).

Thus, a potential strategy to increase retention and completion is to focus on students' resilience and mental health. This chapter considers how college health providers and student affairs professionals can address the relationship between low rates of persistence and high rates of mental health problems to improve students' well-being and academic success. This chapter describes the connection between resilience, mental health, and retention and provides practical implications for campus professionals.

NEW DIRECTIONS FOR STUDENT SERVICES, no. 156, Winter 2016 © 2016 Wiley Periodicals, Inc.
Published online in Wiley Online Library (wileyonlinelibrary.com) • DOI: 10.1002/ss.20194

The Bigger Picture of Retention Efforts

Increasing retention and graduation rates has been a major focus in higher education for decades. Research and policy have emphasized a wide variety of factors, but rarely mental health. Tinto's (1975) classic theory of retention emphasized academic and social integration into institutional communities. Revisions of this framework (Braxton, Hirschy, & McClendon, 2011; Hurtado & Carter, 1997; Kuh, Cruce, Shoup, Kinzie, & Gonyea, 2008) and complementary theories (Bean & Eaton, 2000) emphasize factors such as engagement on campus (Kuh et al., 2008), academic preparation (Adelman, 1999; Tierney, Colyar, & Corwin, 2003), and tuition pricing and financial aid (Chen & DesJardins, 2010; Heller, 2003; John, Paulsen, & Starkey, 1996).

Many of today's retention strategies promote objectives related to these frameworks: (a) providing support for the academic and social transition to college, (b) integrating academic support within daily learning, (c) assessing and monitoring academic risk factors, and (d) engaging students in communities that foster intellectual and social connection (Tinto, 2004). In each of these objectives, faculty and other academic personnel play essential roles as advisors and instructors (Light, 2004). In some cases, students may be persisting because of how they are facing and working through challenges related to their mental health. The connection between resilience and mental health may be an implicit pathway by which programs exert their beneficial effects on retention, but these pathways are rarely an explicit part of the dialogue.

Why Resilience and Mental Health Matter for Retention

Resilience is not merely a natural ability; a person can develop new or stronger resilience skills (Masten, 2001). Factors that enhance resilience include social support, physical health, self-regulation, cognitive flexibility, and optimism (Howard, Dryden, & Johnson, 1999). The ability of students to cope with the inevitable challenges of college life has significant implications for both well-being and academic success. Resilience has benefits that relate to persistence and to the ability of a student to recover from challenges related to mental health. Students who are resilient depend on this strength as a central determinant of mental health. Resilience allows people to maintain or recover good mental health in the face of adversity. Resilience is also an important determinant of academic performance (Leary & DeRosier, 2012); it allows students to persist through and bounce back from academic challenges, such as failing an exam.

Decreasing resilience appears to be contributing factor to a steady decline in mental health in college populations (Eagan, Lozano, Hurtado, & Case, 2013). This trend is not limited to recent years. Depression and anxiety have been rising steadily for many decades, according to a meta-analysis of studies using the Minnesota Multiphasic Personality Inventory (Twenge et al., 2010). This study notes that an increasing focus among young people on extrinsic motivations, such as status, grades, and money, along with impossibly high expectations for these goals, are probably contributing to the negative trends in resilience and mental health. In other words, young people are in a constant state of vulnerability if they are fixated on objectives that are largely outside their own control. These high external expectations can decrease their motivation and ability to overcome barriers.

To summarize our basic conceptual framework. First, we theorize that resilience can directly affect academic outcomes such as retention by influencing how students handle academic challenges and setbacks. Second, we posit that resilience can positively or negatively influence retention indirectly depending on how the student works through and faces mental health challenges. How a student copes with mental health challenges could affect retention by detracting from students' ability and motivation to complete schoolwork, making it less likely they will obtain good grades and persist to graduation. Specifically, poor mental health could decrease students' energy and concentration in school, which may reduce accrual of both real skills and outward signals (such as high grades) that increase expected job opportunities and productivity. Also, conditions such as depression can make students pessimistic about their futures, reducing their motivation to make long-term investments like schooling. Depression is associated with gaps in enrollment of a semester or more (referred to as discontinuous enrollment) (Arria et al., 2013) and a twofold increase in risk of departure from college without graduating (Eisenberg, Golberstein, & Hunt, 2009). There is mounting evidence that how a student uses resilience to cope with mental health is an important determinant of retention and academic performance (Hartley, 2011).

Promising Programs and Initiatives

In recognition of the importance of the relationship between resilience and mental health in college populations, a growing number of programs target these issues and therefore have potential to boost retention. In addition, there are some integrated programs that explicitly address the intersection of resilience, mental health, and academic success. These approaches typically involve collaboration across campus units, including health, academic, and other support services, and they represent a move toward a proactive model that promotes health and well-being as part of the institutional culture and routine. In this section, we describe several such programs. As a way of organizing this discussion, we follow a public health framework, moving from the tertiary level (programs targeting students already experiencing significant mental health and/or academic problems), to the secondary level (programs targeting students with risk factors or emerging risk), to the primary level (programs reaching entire populations).

Tertiary Level. Many new programs are reaching students online, in recognition of the fact that students with mental health struggles do not necessarily access traditional mental health services. For example, the American Foundation for Suicide Prevention's Interactive Screening Program (ISP) uses a web-based screen to identify students with elevated mental health risk and connect them with information and resources (www.afsp.org/our-work/the-interactive-screening-program). The ISP has been implemented on hundreds of campuses across the country. Another online screening-linkage program, eBridge (electronic bridge to mental health), is currently conducting a multisite randomized trial, funded by the National Institutes of Health, in which academic and mental health outcomes are being assessed. eBridge demonstrated promising results in a pilot study; students randomized to online motivational interviewing were more likely to access mental health services (King et al., 2015).

From Intention to Action (FITA) is an integrated program with the explicit goal of addressing both mental health and retention (carleton.ca/fita). This intensive counseling program developed at Carleton University (Ottawa, Canada) targets students who are at risk for academic failure and may be experiencing mental health problems. The program involves 12 weekly meetings with a FITA coordinator, focusing on bolstering well-being and academic performance. Students who began FITA with poor mental health have had improvements in both mental health and course grades, allowing them to avoid academic suspension (Meissner & Konecki, 2015).

Peer-based programs have also increased in popularity as an approach to support distressed students. Since 2007, the Student Support Network at Worcester Polytechnic Institute has trained hundreds of students to help peers in crisis (www.wpi.edu/offices/sdcc/student-network.html).

Secondary Level. A widely implemented model for students at risk for dropping out is the Student Support Services (SSS) Program. This U.S. Department of Education initiative serves two highly vulnerable populations: low-income, first-generation students and students with disabilities who demonstrate academic need (www2.ed.gov/programs/triostudsupp/index.html). Institutions apply for federal funding to administer an SSS program, which provides participants with academic tutoring, close advising, and holistic personal, career, and financial counseling. With their holistic approach, SSS programs could naturally extend to promoting mental health and resilience more explicitly.

The Penn Resiliency Program, at the University of Pennsylvania, focuses specifically on mental health. Their curriculum and programming have developed over 25 years and use principles and practices of cognitive behavioral therapy to support students who may be vulnerable to stress-related mental illness. Their program model has had wide impact, estimated at more than 30,000 individuals, by both providing direct services to students and by training people to teach resilience-related skills (https://ppc.sas.upenn.edu/services/penn-resilience-training).

Primary Level.   On a primary/universal level, curriculum-based approaches can reach entire cohorts of students at an institution during certain key periods. Many campuses have designed first-year experience (FYE) programs to foster holistic student development and a healthy college transition. FYE programs include a wide range of initiatives, such as summer orientations, first-year seminars, peer- or faculty-led support groups, and targeted advising. Although there are some mixed findings regarding the impact of FYE programs (Robbins, Oh, Le, & Button, 2009), in general these programs are considered a "high-impact educational practice" according to the Association of American Colleges and Universities (Kuh, 2008), and participation is associated in many studies with successful outcomes (Pascarella & Terenzini, 2005). Programs commonly focus on practical and academic (e.g., course scheduling) aspects of college life (Hunter, 2006; Padgett & Keup, 2011), with minimal emphasis on stress, coping, and resilience (Leary & DeRosier, 2012), however.

A promising first-year seminar with a focus on resilience and mental health has begun through a research study at University of Nevada-Reno. Students were randomized to an online program based on Acceptance and Commitment Therapy (ACT) or to a waitlist control. The program, ACT on College Life (ACT-CL), targeted cognitive flexibility to prevent a range of mental health problems. ACT-CL decreased depression and anxiety among students with at least minimal baseline distress (Levin, Pistorello, Seeley, & Hayes, 2014). Another notable curriculum-based initiative is SCoRE (Student Curriculum on Resilience Education), a program designed to help students cope with personal, social, and academic challenges (www.scoreforcollege.org). Incorporating online self-reflections, activities, and personalized reports, SCoRE aims to strengthen resilience so that students can adjust to and persist in the face of adversity.

Another way of thinking about primary approaches is to consider the underlying campus culture and its impact on student well-being, resilience, and retention. In some cases, teaching pedagogies and grading policies may need to be reexamined. Practices such as grading on a curve can engender competition and stifle opportunities for collaborative learning (Fines, 1996; Hurtado et al., 2011). Likewise, certain instructional contexts, such as large lectures, lack opportunities for the substantive student–faculty interaction which is vital to student engagement (Baldwin, 2009). Several promising programs have been designed to counter these trends and create a more supportive academic climate. For example, the Expert Electronic Coaching (ECoach) program at University of Michigan uses open-source software to provide individualized feedback and advising messages to undergraduates in large, introductory lectures (http://ai.umich.edu/portfolio/e-coach/). Such programs can provide guidance about productively facing challenges and setbacks, and could be enhanced to address resilience and well-being.

Colleges can also help to normalize "failure" as part of the learning process. An interesting example of this is Harvard University's "Reflections on Rejections" (successfailureproject.bsc.harvard.edu/reflections-rejections), a collection of video- and text-based accounts of rejection as experienced by Harvard deans, faculty, students, and alumni. Related to this, mindset interventions developed by social psychologists have potential benefits for resilience, mental health, and retention. The mindsets that students adopt toward ability (Dweck, 2006) and stress (Crum, Salovey, & Achor, 2013) are associated with academic and mental health outcomes in college populations. Finally, peer-based approaches also have potential to be helpful at a primary level. For example, the Wolverine Support Network at University of Michigan organizes weekly discussion groups facilitated by trained peer leaders to address well-being (csg.umich.edu/student-resources/wolverine-support-network).

Strategies and Recommendations

There are exciting opportunities to increase retention rates through greater attention to intentionally nurturing resilience and mental health, as highlighted by the examples described in this chapter. These opportunities are consistent with the general movement toward a more integrated, holistic approach to student wellness and success. In the coming years, we anticipate a wave of new programs and evidence regarding how to increase retention through programs that address the relationship between resilience and mental health. In the meantime, based on our review of current programs and evidence, we recommend that student affairs practitioners and leaders consider adopting, or enhancing, programs that promote student resilience and mental health through a variety of settings beyond the important work already done in counseling and health centers. By implementing these programs at multiple levels, campuses can foster a culture that recognizes the connections between resilience, mental health, and retention. Strategies may include:

- Academic advising is an ideal setting in which to bolster students' resilience skills. Advisors can help students adopt more constructive mindsets about their academic skills and growth, and can also proactively refer students to counseling and other resources that might enhance their coping skills before they reach a point of academic or emotional crisis.
- FYE seminars and other courses can potentially increase resilience on a campuswide level. There is emerging evidence of effectiveness for these types of programs and their beneficial impacts on student retention. Student affairs leaders can actively monitor new developments in this area, and can promote the adoption of courses that build resilience skills.
- Peer support groups can offer an important complement to the services provided by campus professionals. Student affairs leaders should foster

NEW DIRECTIONS FOR STUDENT SERVICES • DOI: 10.1002/ss

the growth and development of these groups and help them implement evidence-based methods for teaching resilience skills.

- Online programs can reach large numbers of students at very low cost. Online screening and referral programs can help struggling students, as described previously, and information promoting resilience for coping with challenges through information shared via e-mail, websites, and social media can help all types of students.

- Student data analytics are increasingly sophisticated in higher education, and have great potential to address resilience, mental health, and retention. A rich variety of sources—such as admissions data, course data, and measures collected from surveys and mobile devices—could provide a full picture of students' academic and overall well-being and offer them real-time resources that fit their needs.

- The provision of comprehensive campus mental health services, as described in Chapter 2, is also essential to fostering student success. Given the connection between mental health, retention, and resilience, it is necessary to have a campus counseling center offering the broad range of prevention and intervention services.

References

Adelman, C. (1999). *Answers in the tool box. Academic intensity, attendance patterns, and bachelor's degree attainment.* Washington, DC: National Institute on Postsecondary Education, Libraries, and Lifelong Learning, Office of Educational Research and Improvement, U.S. Department of Education.

Arria, A. M., Caldeira, K. M., Vincent, K. B., Winick, E. R., Baron, R. A., & O'Grady, K. E. (2013). Discontinuous college enrollment: Associations with substance use and mental health. *Psychiatric Services, 64*(2), 165–172.

Baldwin, R. G. (2009). The climate for undergraduate teaching and learning in STEM fields. *New Directions for Teaching and Learning: No. 117. Improving the climate for undergraduate teaching and learning in STEM fields* (pp. 9–17). San Francisco, CA: Jossey-Bass.

Bean, J. P., & Eaton, S. B. (2000). A psychological model of college student retention. *Reworking the Student Departure Puzzle, 1*, 48–61.

Bound, J., Lovenheim, M., & Turner, S. (2010). Why have college completion rates declined. An analysis of changing student preparation and collegiate resources. *American Economic Journal: Applied Economics, 2*, 129–157.

Bowen, W. G., Chingos, M. M., & McPherson, M. S. (2009). *Crossing the finish line: Completing college at America's public universities.* Princeton, NJ: Princeton University Press.

Braxton, J. M., Hirschy, A. S., & McClendon, S. A. (2011). *Understanding and reducing college student departure* [ASHE-ERIC Higher Education Report, *30*(3)]. San Francisco, CA: Jossey-Bass.

Chen, R., & DesJardins, S. L. (2010). Investigating the impact of financial aid on student dropout risks: Racial and ethnic differences. *Journal of Higher Education, 81*(2), 179–208.

Crum, A. J., Salovey, P., & Achor, S. (2013). Rethinking stress: The role of mindsets in determining the stress response. *Journal of Personality and Social Psychology, 104*(4), 716–733.

Dweck, C. (2006). *Mindset: The new psychology of success.* New York: Random House.

Eagan, K., Lozano, J. B., Hurtado, S., & Case, M. H. (2013). *The American freshman: National norms fall 2013.* Los Angeles: Higher Education Research Institute, UCLA.

Eisenberg, D., Golberstein, E., & Hunt, J. (2009). Mental health and academic success in college. *B.E. Journal of Economic Analysis and Policy, 9*(1), Article 40.

Eisenberg, D., Hunt, J., & Speer, N. (2013). Mental health in American colleges and universities: Variation across student subgroups and across campuses. *Journal of Nervous and Mental Disease, 201*(1), 60–67.

Eiser, A. (2011). The crisis on campus. *Monitor on Psychology, 42*(8), 18.

Fines, B. G. (1996). Competition and the curve. *UMKC Law Review, 65,* 879–915.

Gabriel, T. (2010, December 9). Mental health needs seen growing at colleges. *New York Times.*

Hartley, M. T. (2011). Examining the relationships between resilience, mental health, and academic persistence in undergraduate college students. *Journal of American College Health, 59*(7), 596–604.

Heller, D. (2003). *Informing public policy: Financial aid and student persistence.* Boulder, CO: Western Interstate Commission for Higher Education.

Howard, S., Dryden, J., & Johnson, B. (1999). Childhood resilience: Review and critique of literature. *Oxford Review of Education, 25*(3), 307–323.

Hunter, M. S. (2006). Fostering student learning and success through first-year programs. *Peer Review, 8*(3), 4–7.

Hurtado, S., & Carter, D. F. (1997). Effects of college transition and perceptions of the campus racial climate on Latino college students' sense of belonging. *Sociology of Education, 70*(4), 324–345.

Hurtado, S., Eagan, M. K., Tran, M. C., Newman, C. B., Chang, M. J., & Velasco, P. (2011). "We do science here": Underrepresented students' interactions with faculty in different college contexts. *Journal of Social Issues, 67*(3), 553–579.

John, E. S., Paulsen, M. B., & Starkey, J. B. (1996). The nexus between college choice and persistence. *Research in Higher Education, 37*(2), 175–220.

Kena, G., Aud, S., Johnson, F., Wang, X., Zhang, J., Rathbun, A., ... Kristapovich, P. (2014). *The condition of education 2014 (NCES 2014–083).* Washington, DC: National Center for Education Statistics.

King, C. A., Eisenberg, D., Zheng, K., Czyz, E., Kramer, A., Horwitz, A., & Chermack, S. (2015). Online suicide risk screening and intervention with college students: A pilot randomized controlled trial. *Journal of Consulting and Clinical Psychology, 83*(3), 630—636.

Kuh, G. D. (2008). *High-impact educational practices: What they are, who has access to them, and why they matter.* Washington, DC: Association of American Colleges and Universities.

Kuh, G. D., Cruce, T. M., Shoup, R., Kinzie, J., & Gonyea, R. M. (2008). Unmasking the effects of student engagement on first-year college grades and persistence. *Journal of Higher Education, 79*(5), 540–563.

Leary, K. A., & DeRosier, M. E. (2012). Factors promoting positive adaptation and resilience during the transition to college. *Psychology, 3*(12), 1215–1222.

Levin, M., Pistorello, J., Seeley, J. R., & Hayes, S. C. (2014). Feasibility of a prototype web-based acceptance and commitment therapy prevention program for college students. *Journal of American College Health, 62*(1), 20–30.

Light, R. J. (2004). *Making the most of college: Students speak their minds.* Cambridge, MA: Harvard University Press.

Masten, A. S. (2001). Ordinary magic: Resilience processes in development. *American Psychologist, 56*(3), 227–238.

Meissner, J., & Konecki, R. (2015). *Annual report of Carleton University's FIT: Action program.*

Padgett, R. D., & Keup, J. R. (2011). *2009 national survey of first-year seminars: Ongoing efforts to support students in transition.* Columbia, SC: National Resource Center for the First-Year Experience and Students in Transition, University of South Carolina.

Pascarella, E. T., & Terenzini, P. T. (2005). *How college affects students: A third decade of research* (Vol. 2). San Francisco, CA: Jossey-Bass.

Robbins, S. B., Oh, I., Le, H., & Button, C. (2009). Intervention effects on college performance and retention as mediated by motivational, emotional, and social control factors: Integrated meta-analytic path analyses. *Journal of Applied Psychology, 94*(5), 1163–1184.

Schwartz, V., & Kay, J. (2009). The crisis in college and university mental health. *Psychiatric Times, 26*(10), 32–32.

Snyder, T. D., & Dillow, S. A. (2013). *Digest of education statistics, 2012 (NCES 2014–015).* Washington, DC: National Center for Education Statistics.

Tierney, W. G., Colyar, J. E., & Corwin, Z. B. (2003). *Preparing for college: Building expectations, changing realities.* Los Angeles: University of Southern California, Center for Higher Education Policy Analysis. Retrieved from ERIC database. (ED482059)

Tinto, V. (1975). Dropout from higher education: A theoretical synthesis of recent research. *Review of Educational Research, 45*(1), 89–125.

Tinto, V. (2004). *Student retention and graduation: Facing the truth, living with the consequence.* (Occasional paper 1). Washington, DC: Pell Institute for the Study of Opportunity in Higher Education.

Twenge, J. M., Gentile, B., DeWall, C. N., Ma, D., Lacefield, K., & Schurtz, D. R. (2010). Birth cohort increases in psychopathology among young Americans, 1938–2007: A cross-temporal meta-analysis of the MMPI. *Clinical Psychology Review, 30*(2), 145–154.

DANIEL EISENBERG *is an associate professor of health management and policy at the University of Michigan.*

SARAH KETCHEN LIPSON *is a doctoral student in public health and higher education at the University of Michigan.*

JULIE POSSELT *is an assistant professor of education at the University of Southern California.*

The provision of college mental health services is undergoing a dynamic evolution. The ability of mental health practitioners and administrators to balance multiple and sometimes opposing trends may determine the future course of mental health services in higher education.

Anticipating the Future of Mental Health Needs on Campus

Robert A. Bonfiglio

Each new academic year seems to bring with it new issues related to the seemingly Sisyphean task of proving ample mental health services and support. In developing this chapter, several observations were gleaned from the daily challenges of managing student well-being that will bear additional consideration as college and university mental health services evolve in the 21st century. These challenges stem from a number of trends that have emerged over the past decade, and even within the past few years, that are having a significant impact on both our campuses as a whole and student mental health. They have been compounded by a more aggressive approach to risk management among college and university administrators and increasing awareness, and perhaps even understanding of, mental illness in American society.

Observations from the Field

Aside from the specific mental health issues with which students are dealing, there are several overarching themes that are likely to increasingly shape campus services and programs related to student mental health. These include the ways in which identities (both students' and professionals') frame experience, the importance of counseling center engagement with the campus community, and the increasing focus on institutional risk management.

The Fluidity of Identity. We live in a time where the fluidity of personal identity, including gender identity, is seemingly more acknowledged than ever before. Identifying, clarifying, and developing one's personal identity remains one of the fundamental personal challenges experienced by college and university students. Surely, the experimentation and variability

New Directions for Student Services, no. 156, Winter 2016 © 2016 Wiley Periodicals, Inc.
Published online in Wiley Online Library (wileyonlinelibrary.com) • DOI: 10.1002/ss.20195

of identity seen in college-going young adults is likely to continue to be discussed, played out, and reflected upon on college and university campuses and in their counseling centers. Although anxiety, depression, and relationship issues have for many years topped the list of reasons for students to engage college and university mental health providers, it would seem that identity formation questions will bring greater numbers of students into college and university counseling centers in the foreseeable future and generate questions and concerns that will resonate across campuses.

Identity development, intellectual development and social development are three interrelated expected outcomes of higher learning. In many cases, college and university mental health providers are the identity development experts on their campuses. These staff members will be expected to take a leadership role in facilitating an institutionwide understanding of the developmental challenges faced by college and university students, especially as they pertain to visible changes in students' social identities.

Counselor Diversity. In the wake of the Black Lives Matter movement, campus activism related to the support and full integration of students of color into the campus experience has brought attention to the lack of availability of mental health professionals on college and university campuses from underrepresented racial groups. Just as in college and university faculties and staffs, changes in the composition of college-going groups have not been mirrored by changes in the composition of the counseling profession. For example, in 2013, among all working psychologists, the percentage of Black/African American psychologists active in the workplace (not only in higher education) was 5.3% (American Psychological Association, 2015). Because this accounts for all working psychologists, it can be assumed that the percentage working in higher education counseling services is significantly smaller.

Given the basic nature of the counselor–student relationship, and the issues of trust building inherent in it, there is an acute need for the counseling profession to more intentionally consider and take action on the demographic makeup of the college and university mental health counseling profession. Similarly, all counselors from various backgrounds and identities must be able to extend their ability to best serve international students; students from diverse religious groups; and lesbian, gay, bisexual, transgender, queer; and other identity groups. Regardless of the counselors' own identities, it is critical that all counseling staff be actively involved in the necessary work to build and sustain intercultural competence. College student populations are changing, and the failure to address the issue of the composition and makeup of college and university mental health care staffs will likely constrain the ability of these staff members to meet the needs of the 21st century college and university student.

Outreach Is Critical. College and university mental health counselors who rely on the philosophy of "if you build it they will come" will also likely find that they are missing out on serving key segments of the college-going populace. Awareness and marketing of counseling services require more than a website and word of mouth; student well-being is best supported through a high-touch environment. George Kuh and his colleagues (1994) have written on the importance of "human scale settings characterized by ethics of membership and care" (p. 58) as key components of student success. Such expectations for human scale settings require college and university mental health counselors to connect with students where students typically are, and the vast majority of our students are not typically found in college and university counseling centers. If counselors are confined solely to their offices and are not out among students who are not their clients they will be less likely to connect with students who have not taken advantage of college mental health services.

It may be difficult to reconcile this need with the reality of the extremely high demand for college and university counseling that require counselors to staff their offices during every available counseling slot. Nonetheless, it is crucial for college and university mental health providers to be seen as active, accessible campus citizens. The ingenuity and creativity of college and university mental health administrators will be tested to resolve this issue and promote the kind of student–staff interaction that has been documented to promote student success.

Police Public Safety Role College University Mental Health.   Because taking a student into protective custody is one of the tools of the university or college police or public safety department, the relationship between college and university mental health practitioners and the police or public safety officers at their institutions is a critical one. Mental health interventions are, at their essence, community interventions, and the engagement of police or public safety officers in the area of mental health should never be unilateral. It is important for mental health service providers and college and university law enforcement and public safety officials to engage each other prior to calls to action to address mental health concerns. In the event of a protective custody situation, any decisions that are not made collaboratively run the risk of placing two departments at odds with each other and placing students in the middle of interdepartmental conflict.

It is imperative that campus police or public safety and mental health services providers are on the same page about how to address student behaviors that are manifestations of students' mental health challenges. Protocols developed proactively in partnership between law enforcement or public safety departments and health and counseling departments are critical to effectively managing mental health emergencies. In addition, the joint training of university and college police or public safety officials and counseling services personnel on student mental health issues, and the inclusion of other institutional staff in such areas as residence life, must be a high priority for college and university mental health care givers.

Risk Management as an Operational Philosophy.   As we look to the future of college and university mental health services, there are two current trends that may dictate the direction these services take. One is the seemingly ever-increasing need for our institutions to engage in risk management. Thomas Miller and Roger Sorochty, in their recently published book *Risk Management in Student Affairs: Foundations for Safety and Success*, state that "It is almost certain that risk management challenges for student affairs administrators will occur with increased frequency in the future" (2015, p. 230). If we define risk management as "the identification, analysis, assessment, control, and avoidance, minimization, or elimination of unacceptable risks" (BusinessDictionary.comBusinessDictionary.com, n.d.), one wonders what mental health conditions college and university administrators may deem as presenting unacceptable risks, and what actions college and university mental health service providers might be compelled to take when confronted with students with complex mental health issues so they might avoid, minimize, or eliminate risk.

Certainly, whenever a counselor or therapist is dealing with clients with mental health challenges risk exists. And although rubrics may be available to help determine acceptable levels of risk, the reliability of such tools can be questionable. If risk management continues to rise in prominence as an overriding approach to institutional management, it would seem likely that services to students would become constrained. However, given that students with mental health challenges do exist on our campuses, it may be a greater risk not to treat these students.

Student affairs work in general, and student mental health counseling in particular, is rife with risk. If minimizing risk becomes an overriding institutional priority, it is entirely possible that colleges and universities might seek to eliminate inherently perilous enterprises such as college mental health counseling. Especially in communities where options for mental health services are readily available, risk-averse administrators may opt to eliminate campus-based services and transfer said risk to community-based service providers. The reliance on community-based service providers as a substitute for campus mental health services would seem to be a deterrent to an integrated approach to student development that includes a campus-wide safety net of student support. Reliance on community-based service providers would also mean that students are receiving services from clinicians with limited knowledge about the campus culture and realities, and that the campus community (particularly faculty and staff) would have limited opportunities to consult with mental health professionals about students of concern.

Growing Awareness of Mental Health Issues

A trend that may dramatically affect student mental health services in the future is greater levels of transparency about mental illness in American society. In Chapter 2, Locke, Wallace, and Brunner describe the relative silence that has characterized American society's response to the increased prevalence of mental and behavioral health issues. There are some signs, however, that seem to hint at the nearing of a tipping point that may result in breaking this silence.

Even though mental illness is still not well understood both on a scientific and a social level, in recent years, there seems to be less societal guardedness around issues of mental health. Witness in popular culture the reception to such films as *The Silver Linings Playbook*, television shows as *Monk*, and the best-selling book somehow turned into a compelling night of theater called *The Curious Incident of the Dog in the Night*. These works have all exposed issues of mental illness more broadly and have fostered dialogue on the nature of mental illness and the treatment of the mentally ill. Witness as well the increasing prevalence at both ends of life's spectrum of two confounding mental health challenges—autism and Alzheimer's disease—and how the widespread presence of these illnesses have left few families unfamiliar with these challenging conditions.

Exposure and experience breed empathy and acceptance, and although a tendency toward risk management may work against supporting students challenged with mental health issues to the fullest extent, the trend of greater exposure to people with mental health challenges may lead to great empathy for students dealing with these challenges. Those administrators and service providers coming to issues of student mental health with exposure to these matters may bring a more humanistic approach to their work and make decisions based less on contractual agreements and more on a truly humane duty to care.

An Ethic of Care

As Richard P. Keeling (2014) puts it in the article "An Ethic of Care in Higher Education: Well-Being and Learning," "advancing student success requires attention to students as whole people, and to their individual and collective well-being. Attention to students as whole people, a shared responsibility for learning, and responsiveness to students' well-being, taken together, reflect the existence and influence of an underlying ethic of care" (p. 141). Keeling goes on to write that: "An ethic of care requires that colleges and universities recognize, acknowledge, and manage or overcome individual, community, and systematic challenges and barriers to students' well-being" (p. 146).

We seem to be living in a time where we are willing, in some cases, to go to extraordinary lengths to ensure individual safety. In working with students, although safety is an essential condition for student learning so too is risk. As Margaret Healy and her colleagues remind us in "The Role of the Campus Professional as a Moral Mentor" (2012), "developmental theorists have long acknowledged the necessity of challenge to facilitate developmental growth" (p. 85), and "it is through discomfort that transformative learning may occur" (p. 85). Because learning often results from risks taken and challenge entails risk, the avoidance, minimization, or elimination of risk in college and university mental health services seems highly unlikely. The tension between our wanting to keep students as safe as possible, and our desire to manage risk, with our desire to promote student independence, development, and learning is, in our view, one of the major challenges those of us who work with college and university students are facing in the 21st century. It would be a monumental disservice to our students if we were to consistently choose the safest, least controversial, or least upsetting path when making administrative decisions. Such a choice, in fact, would be counter to student learning and development.

Balancing Risk and Care

The tension between risk management and student development is but one of a number of tensions that are present in a dynamic campus community. In *Creating Campus Community: In Search of Ernest Boyer's Legacy*, Grady Bogue (2002) notes that a "healthy community is one in which essential but often competing values are maintained in tensioned balance—the balance between access and excellence in education, rights and responsibility, justice and mercy, diversity and community, opportunity and disciplined effort, cooperation and competition, service and profit, self-interest and self-sacrifice, tradition and innovation" (p. 3). Without that balance, according to Bogue, "community degenerates" (p. 3). Bogue concludes that "orchestrating the tension between individual interests and community interests, between the good of self and the good of the community" (p. 5) requires great engagement.

When providing mental health services, the tension between individual interests and community interests is manifested in the tension between offering earnest empathy and support and aggressively managing institutional risk. Orchestrating this tension will likely be one of the most significant challenges not only for the providers of student mental health services on college and university campuses but also for many other college and university faculty and staff as well. This challenge will no doubt require our complete attention, and a multitude of skills.

The metaphor of an orchestra is quite apt for considering how we might proceed in the future. The League of American Orchestras (n.d.) has identified the traits and skills of an effective music conductor, including mastery of technical skills, mastery of interpretive skills and instincts, inquisitiveness, an expansive base of knowledge of the field, practical experience, and thorough grounding in professional ethics.

These are the same skills that come into play when orchestrating the balance between individual interests and community interests to best serve the needs of students with mental health challenges. Imagine the harmony both our students and our institutions will generate if we are able to effectively bring about this balance—recognizing and acting on the need for risk management, and also ensuring that our empathy and commitment to an "ethic of care" is not subordinated to that need. The magnitude of this challenge is commensurate with the magnitude of the contributions college and university mental health practitioners make to some students' college experiences. We are called to embrace this challenge, as it is in keeping with the values and aims that are at the heart of student affairs work in higher education.

Strategies and Recommendations

In many ways, the future of college and university mental health services will be determined by the willingness of college and university leaders to make student mental health an institutional priority, and for all of those who teach and work with students to bring that priority to life. More specifically, there are several intentions and actions related to the issues examined in this chapter that may provide a path forward for those engaged in developing college and university mental health policies and programs.

- Colleges and universities already have their own in-house experts in the field of student development in their counseling centers. College and university mental health staff members must be called upon to actively share their expertise to facilitate an institutionwide understanding of the developmental challenges faced by college and university students, especially as they pertain to visible changes in students' social identities.
- College and university leaders are highly encouraged to support the efforts of college and university mental health services professionals who are committed to taking action to diversify the demographic makeup of their mental health provider staff.
- All counseling staff members must be actively involved in building and sustaining professional intercultural competence.
- Institutional leaders are strongly advised to enable college and university mental health practitioners to have opportunities to actively participate in the activities of the institution beyond merely the provision of counseling services and become more fully integrated into the institutional culture.
- Active collaboration between institutional police or public safety officials and college and university mental health services providers must come to be expected when protocols and training opportunities related to student mental health are developed.
- The facilitation of learning always requires the active management of risk. Risk management is inherent in providing mental health services, yet it must not be the sole determinant of institutional decision-making related to student mental health. Institutional decision makers and mental health providers will be challenged to manage individual and institutional risks judiciously.

NEW DIRECTIONS FOR STUDENT SERVICES • DOI: 10.1002/ss

Campus mental health counselors and the administrators responsible for these services can take the lead in fostering a campuswide ethic of care and maintaining a balanced approach to institutional risk. In the end, how students with mental health issues are served across an institution may come to be a litmus test for an institution's commitment to its core values. As pointed out by Paula Krebs (2015, paragraph 5), "ultimately, as faculty, staff, or administrators, we cannot make every decision purely on the basis of kindness or empathy. But if we start from there, it is easier to get to a good decision."

References

American Psychological Association. (2015). 2005–13: Demographics of the U.S. psychology workforce. Retrieved from http://www.apa.org/workforce/publications/13-dem-acs/index.aspx

Bogue, E. G. (2002). An agenda of common caring: The call for community in higher education. In W. M. McDonald (Ed.), Creating campus community: In search of Ernest Boyer's legacy. San Francisco: Jossey-Bass.

BusinessDictionary.com. (n.d.). Risk management. Retrieved from http://www.businessdictionary.com/definition/risk-management.html

Healy, M. A., Lancaster, J. M., Liddell, D. L., & Stewart, D. L. (2012). The role of the campus professional as a moral mentor. In D. L. Liddell & D. L. Cooper (Eds.), New Directions for Student Services: No. 139. Facilitating the moral growth of college students (pp. 83–92). San Francisco: Jossey-Bass.

Keeling, R. P. (2014). An ethic of care in higher education: Well-being and learning. Journal of College and Character, 15(3), 141–148.

Krebs, P. (2015, April 14). "Everyone is cranky lately." Chronicle Vitae. Retrieved from https://chroniclevitae.com/news/974-everyone-is-cranky-lately

Kuh, G. D., Douglas, K. B., Lund, J. P., & Ramin-Gyurnek, J. (1994). Student learning outside the classroom: Transcending artificial boundaries [ASHE-ERIC Higher Education Report No. 8]. Washington, DC: The George Washington University Graduate School of Education and Human Development.

League of American Orchestras. (n.d.). Traits and skills of a music director. Retrieved from http://www.americanorchestras.org/conducting-artistic-programs/conducting/traits-and-skills-of-a-music-director.html

Miller, T. E., & Sorochty, R. W. (2015). Risk management in student affairs: Foundations for safety and success. San Francisco: Jossey-Bass.

ROBERT A. BONFIGLIO is vice president for student and campus life at the State University of New York at Geneseo.

INDEX